GREATEST EVER

Salads

p

This is a Parragon Publishing Book
First published in 2005

Parragon Publishing
Queen Street House
4 Queen Street
Bath BA1 1HE, UK

ISBN: 1-40545-384-2

Printed in Indonesia

Photography and text by The Bridgewater Book Company Ltd

NOTE

Cup measurements in this book are for American cups. This book also uses
imperial and metric measurements. Follow the same units of measurement
throughout; do not mix imperial and metric.
All spoon measurements are level: teaspoons are assumed to be 5 ml and
tablespoons are assumed to be 15 ml. Unless otherwise stated, milk is assumed
to be whole milk, eggs and individual vegetables such as potatoes are medium,
and pepper is freshly ground black pepper.

The times given for each recipe are an approximate guide only because the
preparation times may differ according
to the techniques used by different people and the cooking times may vary as
a result of the type of oven used.

Recipes using raw or very lightly cooked eggs should be
avoided by infants, the elderly, pregnant women, convalescents, and anyone
suffering from an illness.

Contents

Introduction

Salads are not just for summer but for all year round.

They can be crisp and light, stimulating and spicy, or

substantial and satisfying. Imagine tempting appetizers,

complementary accompaniments, refreshing palate

cleansers, and filling main courses. Nor should we

forget that fruit salads make delicious desserts!

In the first century, the Roman scientist Pliny described nine different kinds

of lettuce, but he would be amazed by the range and variety of salad leaves

available today. He certainly would not have been able to imagine the

dozens of other ingredients that are now combined to make luscious salads;

mushrooms, pasta, rice, couscous, vegetables, pulses, and fruit, not to

mention the meat, poultry, fish, seafood, eggs, and cheese that often take

the starring role in main course salads.

The recipes in this book cover all kinds of salads for every imaginable occasion,

from seasons of the year, to courses on a menu. They have been inspired by both traditional and contemporary dishes from around the world and include classics, family favorites, traditional themes with a new twist, exotic salads, and innovative ideas. A range that extends from Shrimp Cocktail (see page 24) to Buckwheat Noodle Salad with Smoked Tofu (see page149).

The recipes have been divided into six chapters for easy reference. Light Salads is the place to look for quick and easy snacks and fabulous appetizers. Some of the recipes are vegetarian while others feature shrimp, ham, or bacon. Meat Salads offers a mouthwatering collection of main course dishes, some subtle and elegant, some robust and earthy, and others tongue-tingling and spicy. Fish & Seafood Salads includes many of the world's most popular salads, featuring fresh and smoked fish, shrimp, mussels, and even lobster. Vegetarian Salads are among the most imaginative, based around a wide choice of ingredients from cheese and nuts to pasta and lentils. Side Salads not only shows that this popular accompaniment can be so much more than a heap of lettuce, but also how easy it is to team complementary flavors with your chosen main course. Last, but certainly not least, Fruit Salads offer a veritable cornucopia of fresh-tasting desserts.

Salad Basics

The essential quality of salads, whatever their ingredients, is freshness. This is, of course, especially important with salad leaves, as there is little more unappetizing than limp lettuce, but it applies equally to everything else that is included in a salad, such as vegetables, fruit, cheese, nuts, and the oils used in dressings.

Salad Leaves

Look for firm leaves of good color with no signs of browning or slime. They should be used within about two days of purchase, although very crisp lettuces, such as Iceberg and Bibb, can be stored in the salad drawer of the refrigerator for up to five days. It is worth noting that bags of mixed leaves have been treated with oxygen to prolong their shelf life, but once the bag has been opened, they deteriorate very rapidly. The oxygen treatment also reduces their nutritional value significantly, so be sure to combine them with untreated leaves. To prepare, discard any coarse or wilted outer leaves and carefully wash the remainder in cold water. Drain well and then dry in a salad spinner or by wrapping them in a clean dish towel. This is important, as oil-based dressings will not adhere to wet leaves.

Dressings

A basic dressing is essential for a good salad. Good olive oil and a fine vinegar or lemon juice should be used. For the simplest dressing, just sprinkle on some freshly squeezed lemon juice and some olive oil. If you are preparing a salad well in advance, it is usually best not to add the dressing until you are ready to serve. Salad leaves, vegetables, and fruit often wilt and go soggy if the dressing is added too soon. This is not a problem with most pasta, rice, and grain salads, but be guided by the recipe.

Vinaigrette

MAKES ABOUT ⅔ CUP

½ cup olive or other vegetable oil
3 tbsp white wine vinegar or lemon juice
1 tsp Dijon mustard
½ tsp superfine sugar
salt and pepper

1 Put all the ingredients in a screw-top jar, then secure the lid and shake well until a thick emulsion forms. Taste and adjust the seasoning if necessary.

2 Use at once or store in an airtight container in the refrigerator for up to a month. Always whisk or shake the dressing again before using.

Mayonnaise

MAKES ABOUT 1¼ cups

2 large egg yolks
2 tsp Dijon mustard
¾ tsp salt, or to taste
2 tbsp lemon juice or white wine vinegar
about 1¼ cups sunflower-seed oil
white pepper

1 Whiz the egg yolks with the Dijon mustard, salt, and white pepper to taste in a food processor or blender or by hand. Add the lemon juice and whiz again.

2 With the motor still running or still beating, add the oil, drop by drop at first. When the sauce begins to thicken, the oil can then be added in a slow, steady stream. Taste and adjust the seasoning with extra salt, pepper, and lemon juice if necessary. If the sauce seems too thick, slowly add 1 tbsp hot water, light cream, or lemon juice.

3 Use at once or store in an airtight container in the refrigerator for up to 1 week.

Light Salads

With just a few simple ingredients you can rustle up a tasty lunchtime treat in next to no time. This chapter features deliciously refreshing, flavor-packed salads, many of them ideal for anyone watching the calories or following a healthy eating plan. Some of them can even be packed in a plastic box for a sandwich-free lunchtime in the office. It's also full of fabulous ideas for appetizers if you're entertaining, whether your taste is for the classic Figs & Prosciutto (see page 34), the traditional Shrimp Cocktail (see page 24), the exotic Chinese Salad Nests (see page 41), or the imaginative Potato Wedges with Apricot & Walnuts (see page 25). The recipes feature everyone's favorite salad ingredients from tomatoes to beet, as well as some surprisingly delicious new ideas.

mozzarella & tomatoes

serves four

1 lb 5 oz/600 g plum tomatoes

10½ oz/300 g mozzarella cheese

16 fresh basil leaves, torn if large

½ cup extra-virgin olive oil, to serve

1 Using a sharp knife, cut the tomatoes into even slices about ¼ inch/5 mm thick. Drain the mozzarella cheese and discard the whey. Slice the mozzarella cheese evenly.

2 Arrange the tomato and mozzarella slices, overlapping slightly, in concentric circles on a large serving plate.

3 Sprinkle the basil over the salad and serve immediately with the olive oil for drizzling.

COOK'S TIP

If you can find them, use fresh plum tomatoes as they are less watery than the standard round varieties. Try to use sun-ripened tomatoes as they have a richer flavor.

tomato, fennel & apple salad

serves four

1 small fennel bulb

2 large beefsteak tomatoes,
    cut into wedges

1 eating apple, quartered, cored,
    and sliced

6-inch/15-cm piece cucumber,
    peeled

4 tbsp olive oil

2 tbsp lemon juice

½ tsp Dijon mustard

salt and pepper

fennel fronds, to garnish

VARIATION

For a different look, try smaller
baby tomatoes instead of
beefsteak tomatoes.

1 Using a sharp knife, thinly slice
the fennel bulb and place in a
large serving dish with the tomato
wedges and apple slices.

2 Cut the cucumber in half
lengthwise and, using a
teaspoon, scoop out the seeds and
discard. Cut each half into thick slices
and add to the salad.

3 Mix the oil, lemon juice, and
mustard together in a small
bowl. Season to taste with salt and
pepper and pour over the salad. Toss
gently until the salad is coated with the
dressing. Snip the fennel fronds over
the top to garnish and serve.

tomato & pine nut salad

serves four

4 ripe plum tomatoes, coarsely
   chopped

8 oven-dried tomato halves, sliced

1¼ cups arugula leaves

4 tbsp pine nuts

9 oz/250 g provolone cheese,
   drained

3 tbsp olive oil

1 tbsp lemon juice

salt and pepper

warmed pita bread, to serve

1 Preheat the broiler to medium.
Place all the tomatoes in a large
serving dish. Add the arugula leaves
and toss together.

2 Dry-fry the pine nuts in a skillet
until lightly browned, then
sprinkle over the salad.

3 Cut the provolone cheese into
thick slices, then arrange on a
large baking sheet. Place under the hot
broiler and cook until browned on both
sides. Arrange the cheese over the
tomato salad.

4 Mix the oil and lemon juice
together in a small bowl. Season
with salt and pepper and pour over
the salad. Serve at once with warmed
pita bread.

VARIATION

This recipe is also great with
goats cheese which has
a delicious strong taste.

bell pepper salad

serves four

1 onion

2 red bell peppers

2 yellow bell peppers

3 tbsp olive oil

2 large zucchinis, sliced

2 garlic cloves, sliced

1 tbsp balsamic vinegar

1¾ oz/50 g anchovy fillets, chopped

2 tbsp black olives, halved and
    pitted

salt and pepper

1 tbsp chopped fresh basil

TOMATO TOASTS

small stick of French bread

1 garlic clove, crushed

1 tomato, peeled and chopped

2 tbsp olive oil

salt and pepper

1 Cut the onion into wedges. Core and seed the bell peppers and cut into thick slices.

2 Heat the oil in a heavy-bottom skillet. Add the onion, bell peppers, zucchinis, and garlic and cook gently for 20 minutes, stirring occasionally.

3 Add the vinegar, anchovies, olives, and seasoning to taste, mix thoroughly and let cool. Spoon the cooled mixture onto individual plates and sprinkle with the basil.

4 To make the Tomato Toasts, preheat the oven to 425°F/220°C. Cut the French bread diagonally into ½-inch / 1-cm slices. Mix the garlic, tomato, oil, and seasoning together, and spread thinly over each slice of bread.

5 Place the bread on a cookie sheet and bake in the preheated oven for 5–10 minutes, until crisp. Serve with the vegetable salad.

COOK'S TIP

If you find canned anchovies rather too salty, soak them in a saucer of cold milk for 5 minutes, then drain and pat dry with paper towels before using. The milk absorbs the salt.

VARIATION

If you like, chop an eggplant into chunks, sprinkle with salt to draw out the juices, then rinse and add in Step 2 with an extra tablespoonful of oil.

bacon with corn salad

serves six

6–8 tbsp corn oil

8 oz/225 g rindless lean bacon, diced

2 garlic cloves, finely chopped

4 slices of white bread, crusts removed, cut into ½-inch/1-cm cubes

5 tbsp red wine vinegar

1 tbsp balsamic vinegar

2 tsp whole-grain mustard

salt and pepper

8 oz/225 g corn salad

1 Heat 2 teaspoons of the corn oil in a large, heavy-bottom skillet. Add the bacon and cook over medium heat, stirring frequently, for 5 minutes, or until crisp. Remove from the skillet with a slotted spoon and drain on paper towels. Add the garlic and diced bread to the skillet and cook, stirring and tossing frequently, until crisp and golden brown on all sides. Remove from the skillet with a slotted spoon and drain on paper towels.

2 Place the red wine vinegar, balsamic vinegar, mustard, and remaining corn oil in a screw-top jar and shake vigorously, then pour into a bowl. Alternatively, mix the vinegars and mustard together in a bowl and whisk in the oil until the dressing is creamy. Season to taste with salt and pepper.

3 Add the corn salad and bacon to the dressing and toss to coat. Divide the salad between serving plates, sprinkle with the croutons, and serve.

COOK'S TIP
If you buy corn salad with the root still attached, let it stand in a bowl of iced water for 1 hour to refresh.

tomato, mozzarella & avocado salad

serves four

2 ripe beefsteak tomatoes

5½ oz/150 g fresh mozzarella
    cheese

2 avocados

4 tbsp olive oil

1½ tbsp white wine vinegar

1 tsp coarse grain mustard

salt and pepper

few fresh basil leaves,
    torn into pieces

20 black olives

fresh crusty bread, to serve

COOK'S TIP

This salad is best eaten straight
away to maintain the freshness
of the basil and the color and
firmness of the avocado.

1 Using a sharp knife, cut the
tomatoes into thick wedges
and place in a large serving dish. Drain
the mozzarella cheese and coarsely tear
into pieces. Cut the avocados in half
and remove the pits. Cut the flesh into
slices, then arrange the mozzarella
cheese and avocado with the tomatoes.

2 Mix the oil, vinegar, and mustard
together in a small bowl,
add salt and pepper to taste, then
drizzle over the salad.

3 Sprinkle the basil and olives over
the top and serve at once with
fresh crusty bread.

orecchiette salad with pears & stilton

serves four

9 oz/250 g dried orecchiette

1 head of radicchio, torn into pieces

1 oak leaf lettuce, torn into pieces

2 pears

3 tbsp lemon juice

9 oz/250 g Stilton cheese, diced

scant ½ cup chopped walnuts

4 tomatoes, quartered

1 red onion, sliced

1 carrot, grated

8 fresh basil leaves

2 oz/55 g corn salad

4 tbsp olive oil

3 tbsp white wine vinegar

salt and pepper

COOK'S TIP

The easiest way to emulsify an oil and vinegar dressing is to put the ingredients in a screw-top jar, secure the lid, and shake vigorously. Otherwise, whisk well in a bowl or pitcher.

1 Bring a large heavy-bottom pan of lightly salted water to a boil. Add the pasta, return to a boil, and cook for 8–10 minutes, or until tender but still firm to the bite. Drain, refresh in a bowl of cold water and drain again.

2 Place the radicchio and oak leaf lettuce leaves in a large bowl. Halve the pears, remove the cores, and dice the flesh. Toss the diced pear with 1 tablespoon of lemon juice in a small bowl to prevent discoloration. Top the salad with the Stilton, walnuts, pears, pasta, tomatoes, onion slices, and grated carrot. Add the basil and corn salad.

3 Mix the remaining lemon juice and the olive oil and vinegar together in a measuring cup, then season to taste with salt and pepper. Pour the dressing over the salad, toss, and serve.

VARIATION

Substitute the oak leaf lettuce with escarole and replace the corn salad with arugula or watercress, if you prefer.

red & green salad

serves four

1 lb 7 oz/650 g cooked beet
3 tbsp extra-virgin olive oil
juice of 1 orange
1 tsp superfine sugar
1 tsp fennel seeds
salt and pepper
4 oz/115 g fresh baby spinach
 leaves

1 Using a sharp knife, dice the cooked beet and set aside until required. Heat the olive oil in a small, heavy-bottom pan. Add the orange juice, sugar and fennel seeds and

season to taste with salt and pepper. Stir constantly until the sugar has dissolved.

2 Add the reserved beet to the pan and stir gently to coat. Remove the pan from the heat.

3 Arrange the baby spinach leaves in a large salad bowl. Spoon the warmed beet on top and serve immediately.

COOK'S TIP

To cook beet, trim the leaves and rinse. Cook in a pan of salted water for 1 hour, or until tender. Drain and let cool. Rub off the skin and trim the root.

anchovy & olive salad

serves four

large handful mixed lettuce leaves

12 cherry tomatoes, halved

20 black olives, pitted and halved

6 canned anchovy fillets, drained
    and sliced

1 tbsp chopped fresh oregano

DRESSING

4 tbsp extra-virgin olive oil

1 tbsp white wine vinegar

1 tbsp lemon juice

1 tbsp chopped fresh flatleaf parsley

salt and pepper

wedges of lemon, to garnish

COOK'S TIP

This dish is all about
presentation, so save a couple
of anchovies, olives and
tomatoes to place decoratively
on top of the salad.

1 Prepare all the salad ingredients as per ingredients list. To make the dressing, put all the ingredients into a small bowl, season with salt and pepper, and stir together well.

2 To assemble the salad, arrange the lettuce leaves in a serving dish. Scatter the cherry tomatoes on top, followed by the olives, anchovies, and oregano. Drizzle over the dressing. Serve on individual plates garnished with lemon wedges.

shrimp cocktail

serves four

1 avocado

1 tbsp lemon juice

1 lb 2 oz/500 g cooked shrimp,
    peeled

DRESSING

1 egg

2 tsp sherry vinegar

½ tsp mustard

dash of Worcestershire sauce

pinch of salt

1¼ cups sunflower oil

scant ½ cup tomato catsup

GARNISH

pinch of paprika

thin strips of lemon zest

4 whole cooked shrimp, optional

fresh salad greens, to serve

1 To make the dressing, break the egg into a food processor. Add the vinegar, mustard, Worcestershire sauce, and salt, and process for 15 seconds. While the motor is running, slowly pour the sunflower oil through the feeder tube, until thoroughly incorporated. Transfer the dressing to a large bowl, then stir in the tomato catsup. Cover with plastic wrap and chill in the refrigerator until required.

2 Cut the avocado in half lengthwise, then remove and discard the pit and skin. Cut the flesh into slices, then brush the slices with lemon juice to prevent discoloration.

3 To assemble the salad, take the dressing from the refrigerator, add the avocado and shrimp, and stir gently until coated.

4 Divide the salad greens between large individual serving glasses or bowls. Fill each one with shrimp, then garnish with paprika and lemon zest strips. If using whole shrimp, hang a whole cooked shrimp on the rim of each glass or bowl. Serve immediately.

potato wedges with apricot & walnuts

serves four

2 large potatoes

3 tbsp extra-virgin olive oil
   or walnut oil

1 tbsp white wine vinegar

large pinch of sugar

salt and pepper

½ cup ready-to-eat dried
   apricots, chopped

TO SERVE

salad greens

1 cup broken walnuts

1 Cut each potato into 8 wedges lengthwise. Simmer in a pan with the minimum of salted boiling water for about 10 minutes, or until tender but not falling apart.

2 Meanwhile, put the oil, white wine vinegar, sugar, salt, and pepper in a screw-topped jar and shake together.

3 Drain the cooked potatoes and put in a large bowl. Add the apricots, pour in the dressing, and gently toss together.

4 Arrange the salad greens on a serving dish and add the potato salad. Sprinkle with the walnuts and serve.

COOK'S TIP

If you prepare the dressing in a screw-top jar, you can save it for a couple of days, and when next needed just top up with more oil or vinegar.

sweet potato and bell pepper salad

serves four

2 sweet potatoes, peeled and cut
   into chunks
2 tbsp olive oil
pepper
2 garlic cloves, crushed
1 large eggplant, sliced
2 red bell peppers, seeded and
   sliced
7 oz/200 g mixed salad greens
2 x 5½ oz/150 g mozzarella cheese,
   drained and sliced
whole-wheat bread, to serve
FOR THE DRESSING
1 tbsp balsamic vinegar
1 garlic clove, crushed
3 tbsp olive oil
1 small shallot, finely chopped
2 tbsp chopped mixed fresh herbs,
   such as tarragon, chervil,
   and basil
pepper

1 Preheat the oven to 375°F/190°C. Put the sweet potato chunks into a roasting pan with the oil, pepper to taste, and garlic and toss to combine. Roast in the preheated oven for 30 minutes, or until soft and slightly charred.

2 Meanwhile, preheat the broiler to high. Arrange the eggplant and bell pepper slices on the broiler pan and cook under the preheated broiler, turning occasionally, for 10 minutes, or until soft and slightly charred.

3 To make the dressing, whisk the vinegar, garlic, and oil together in a small bowl and stir in the shallot and herbs. Season to taste with pepper.

4 To serve, divide the salad greens between 4 serving plates and arrange the sweet potato, eggplant, bell peppers, and mozzarella on top. Drizzle with the dressing and serve with whole-wheat bread.

VARIATION
Use a fork or a sharp knife to test if the sweet potato is cooked. By exerting a small amount of pressure the cutlery should easily slide into the potato.

mixed mushroom salad

serves four

3 tbsp pine nuts

2 red onions, cut into chunks

4 tbsp olive oil

2 garlic cloves, crushed

3 slices whole-wheat bread, cubed

7 oz/200 g mixed salad greens

9 oz/250 g cremini mushrooms,
   sliced

5½ oz/150 g shiitake mushrooms,
   sliced

5½ oz/150 g oyster mushrooms, torn

FOR THE DRESSING

1 garlic clove, crushed

2 tbsp red wine vinegar

4 tbsp walnut oil

1 tbsp finely chopped fresh parsley

pepper

1 Preheat the oven to 350°F/180°C. Heat a nonstick skillet over medium heat, add the pine nuts, and cook, turning, until just browned. Tip into a bowl and set aside.

2 Put the onions and 1 tablespoon of the olive oil into a roasting pan and toss to coat. Roast in the preheated oven for 30 minutes.

3 Meanwhile, heat 1 tablespoon of the remaining oil with the garlic in the nonstick skillet over high heat. Add the bread and cook, turning frequently, for 5 minutes, or until brown and crisp. Remove from the skillet and set aside.

4 Divide the salad greens between 4 serving plates and add the roasted onions. To make the dressing, whisk the garlic, vinegar, and oil together in a small bowl. Stir in the parsley and season to taste with pepper. Drizzle over the salad and onions.

5 Heat the remaining oil in a skillet, add the cremini and shiitake mushrooms, and cook for 2–3 minutes, stirring frequently. Add the oyster mushrooms and cook for an additional 2–3 minutes. Divide the hot mushroom mixture between the 4 plates. Sprinkle over the pine nuts and croutons and serve.

red onion, tomato & herb salad

serves four

2 lb/900 g tomatoes, sliced thinly

1 tbsp sugar, optional

salt and pepper

1 red onion, sliced thinly

large handful coarsely chopped
    fresh herbs

DRESSING

2–4 tbsp vegetable oil

2 tbsp red wine vinegar or
    fruit vinegar

1 Slice the tomato then arrange the slices in a shallow bowl. Sprinkle with sugar (if using), salt, and pepper.

2 Chop and separate the onion slices into rings and sprinkle them over the tomatoes. Sprinkle the herbs over the top. Any fresh herbs that are in season can be used—for example, tarragon, sorrel, cilantro, or basil.

3 Place the dressing ingredients in a jar with a screw-top lid. Shake well. Pour the dressing over the salad and mix gently.

4 Cover with plastic wrap and chill for 20 minutes. Remove the salad from the refrigerator 5 minutes before serving, unwrap the dish, and stir gently before setting out on the table.

COOK'S TIP

If preparing this dish in advance make sure you remember to take it out of the fridge in time for it to warm slightly, to room temperature, so that the flavors can be appreciated.

avocado salad

serves four

large handful of radicchio

large handful of arugula

1 small galia melon

2 ripe avocados

1 tbsp lemon juice

7 oz/200 g fontina cheese,
　　cut into bite-size pieces

DRESSING

5 tbsp lemon-flavored or
　　extra-virgin olive oil

1 tbsp white wine vinegar

1 tbsp lemon juice

1 tbsp chopped fresh parsley

COOK'S TIP

To cut the cheese more easily, take
a sharp knife and wipe with a
damp cloth before cutting. This
enables you to slice with less effort.

1 To make the dressing, mix together the oil, vinegar, lemon juice, and parsley in a small bowl.

2 Arrange the radicchio and arugula on serving plates. Cut the melon in half, then seed it, and cut the flesh away from the skin. Discard the skin. Slice the melon flesh and arrange it over the salad greens.

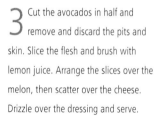

3 Cut the avocados in half and remove and discard the pits and skin. Slice the flesh and brush with lemon juice. Arrange the slices over the melon, then scatter over the cheese. Drizzle over the dressing and serve.

warm red lentil salad with goat cheese

serves four

2 tbsp olive oil

2 tsp cumin seeds

2 garlic cloves, crushed

2 tsp grated fresh gingerroot

1½ cups split red lentils

3 cups vegetable stock

2 tbsp chopped fresh mint

2 tbsp chopped fresh cilantro

2 red onions, thinly sliced

4⅜ cups baby spinach leaves

1 tsp hazelnut oil

5½ oz/150 g soft goat cheese

4 tbsp strained plain yogurt

pepper

1 lemon, cut into quarters,

    to garnish

toasted rye bread, to serve

VARIATION

Warm Ciabatta is a great
accompaniment to this dish, and
makes an interesting alternative
to rye bread.

1 Heat half the olive oil in a large
pan over medium heat, add the
cumin seeds, garlic, and ginger and
cook for 2 minutes, stirring constantly.

2 Stir in the lentils, then add the
stock, a ladleful at a time, until it
is all absorbed, stirring constantly—this
will take about 20 minutes. Remove
from the heat and stir in the herbs.

3 Meanwhile, heat the remaining
olive oil in a skillet over medium
heat, add the onions, and cook, stirring
frequently, for 10 minutes, or until soft
and lightly browned.

4 Toss the spinach in the hazelnut
oil in a bowl, then divide
between 4 serving plates.

5 Mash the goat cheese with the
yogurt in a small bowl and
season to taste with pepper.

6 Divide the lentils between the
serving plates and top with the
onions and goat cheese mixture.
Garnish with lemon quarters and serve
with toasted rye bread.

figs & prosciutto

1½ oz/40 g arugula

4 fresh figs

4 slices prosciutto

4 tbsp olive oil

1 tbsp fresh orange juice

1 tbsp honey

1 small fresh red chili

COOK'S TIP

Chilies can burn the skin
for several hours after chopping,
so it is advisable to wear
gloves when you are handling
any very hot varieties and
to wash your hands.

1 Tear the arugula into manageable pieces and arrange on 4 individual serving plates.

2 Using a sharp knife, cut each of the figs into quarters and place them on top of the arugula leaves.

3 Using a sharp knife, cut the prosciutto into strips and scatter over the rocket and figs.

4 Place the oil, orange juice, and honey in a screw-top jar. Shake the jar vigorously until the mixture emulsifies and forms a thick dressing. Transfer the dressing to a bowl.

5 Using a sharp knife, dice the chili. (You can remove the seeds first if you prefer a milder flavor.) Add the chopped chili to the dressing and mix well.

6 Drizzle the dressing over the prosciutto, arugula, and figs, tossing to mix well. Serve immediately.

capri salad

1 Using a sharp knife, cut the tomatoes into thin slices.

2 Drain the mozzarella, if necessary, and cut into slices.

3 Pit the black olives and slice them into rings.

COOK'S TIP

Buffalo mozzarella cheese has a better flavor than the cow's milk variety. It is popular in salads, but also provides a tangy layer in baked dishes.

4 Layer the tomatoes, mozzarella slices, olives, and basil leaves in a stack, finishing with a layer of cheese on top.

5 Place each stack under a preheated hot broiler for 2–3 minutes or just long enough to melt the mozzarella.

6 Drizzle over the balsamic vinegar and olive oil, and season to taste with a little salt and pepper.

7 Transfer to individual serving plates and garnish with fresh basil leaves. Serve immediately.

sesame seed salad

serves four

1 large eggplant

3 tbsp tahini paste

juice and rind of 1 lemon

1 garlic clove, crushed

pinch of paprika

1 tbsp chopped fresh cilantro

Boston or Bibb lettuce leaves

salt and pepper

GARNISH

strips of pimiento

lemon wedges

toasted sesame seeds

1 Cut the eggplant in half, place in a colander, and sprinkle with salt. Set aside for 30 minutes to allow the juices to drain. Rinse thoroughly under cold running water and drain well. Pat dry with paper towels.

COOK'S TIP

This salad is very versatile and works superbly well with a selection of different nuts and seeds, including pine nuts, sunflower seeds and cashew nuts.

2 Place the eggplant halves, skin side uppermost, on an oiled cookie sheet. Cook in a preheated oven, 450°F/230°C, for 10–15 minutes. Remove from the oven and set aside to cool.

3 When the eggplant is cool enough to handle, cut it into cubes and set aside until required.

4 Combine the tahini paste, lemon juice, lemon rind, garlic, paprika, and chopped cilantro in a medium-size bowl. Season with salt and pepper to taste and stir in the eggplant cubes.

5 Line a serving dish with lettuce leaves and spoon the eggplant cubes into the center. Garnish the salad with pimiento slices, lemon wedges, and toasted sesame seeds and serve immediately.

salad with garlic dressing

serves four

3 oz/85 g cucumber, cut into batons

6 scallions, halved

2 tomatoes, deseeded and cut into
    8 wedges

1 yellow bell pepper, deseeded and
    cut into strips

2 celery stalks, cut into strips

4 radishes, quartered

3 oz/85 g arugula

1 tbsp chopped fresh mint,
    to garnish

DRESSING

2 tbsp lemon juice

1 garlic clove, crushed

⅔ cup lowfat natural yogurt

2 tbsp olive oil

salt and pepper

1 To make the salad, gently mix the cucumber batons, scallions, tomato wedges, yellow bell pepper strips, celery strips, radishes, and arugula in a large serving bowl.

2 To make the dressing, stir the lemon juice, garlic, natural yogurt, and olive oil together in a small bowl they are until thoroughly combined. Season with salt and pepper to taste.

3 Spoon the dressing over the salad and toss to mix. Sprinkle the salad with chopped mint and serve.

COOK'S TIP

Arugula has a distinctive warm, peppery flavor which is ideal in green salads. If arugula is unavailable, mâche makes a good substitute.

mozzarella with radicchio

serves four

1 lb 2 oz/500 g mozzarella cheese

4 large tomatoes, sliced

2 heads of radicchio

fresh basil leaves, to garnish

DRESSING

1 tbsp red or green pesto

6 tbsp extra-virgin olive oil

3 tbsp red wine vinegar

handful of fresh basil leaves

salt and pepper

1 First make the dressing. Whisk together the pesto, olive oil, and red wine vinegar in a small bowl until thoroughly combined.

2 Tear the basil leaves into tiny pieces and add them to the dressing. Season to taste with salt and pepper.

COOK'S TIP

If you are using ready-made pesto, ensure that you buy a good quality brand, with an intense flavor and not too much oil.

3 Thinly slice the mozzarella and arrange it on 4 serving plates with the tomatoes, overlapping the slices.

4 Leaving the root end on the heads of radicchio, slice each one into quarters. Grill them quickly on the barbecue grill, so that the leaves just singe on the outside. Place 2 quarters on each serving plate.

5 Drizzle the dressing over the radicchio, cheese, and tomatoes. Garnish with fresh basil leaves and serve immediately.

chinese salad nests

serves four

POTATO NESTS

2¼ cups grated mealy potatoes

1 cup cornstarch

vegetable oil, for deep-frying

fresh chives, to garnish

SALAD

4½ oz/125 g pineapple, cubed

1 green bell pepper, cut into strips

1 carrot, cut into thin strips

1¾ oz/50 g snow peas, thickly sliced

4 baby corn cobs, halved
  lengthwise

¼ cup bean sprouts

2 scallions, sliced

DRESSING

1 tbsp clear honey

1 tsp light soy sauce

1 garlic clove, crushed

1 tsp lemon juice

1 To make the nests, rinse the potatoes several times in cold water. Drain well on paper towels so they are completely dry. This is to prevent the potatoes spitting when they are cooked in the fat. Place the potatoes in a mixing bowl. Add the cornstarch, mixing well to coat the potatoes.

2 Half fill a wok with vegetable oil and heat until smoking. Line a 6 inch/5 cm diameter wire strainer with a quarter of the potato mixture and press another strainer of the same size on top.

3 Lower the strainers into the oil and cook for 2 minutes until the potato nest is golden brown and crisp. Remove from the wok, allowing the excess oil to drain off.

4 Repeat 3 more times to use up all of the mixture and make a total of 4 nests. Let cool.

5 Mix the salad ingredients together then spoon into the potato baskets.

6 Mix the dressing ingredients together. Pour the dressing over the salad. Garnish with chives and then serve immediately.

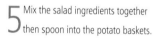

gado gado

serves four

3½ oz/100 g/1 cup shredded
    white cabbage

3½ oz/100 g green beans,
    cut into three

3½ oz/100 g carrots, cut into
    matchsticks

3½ oz/100 g cauliflower florets

3½ oz/100 g bean sprouts

DRESSING

3½ fl oz/100 ml/½ cup vegetable oil

3½ oz/100 g/1 cup unsalted
    peanuts

2 garlic cloves, crushed

1 small onion, finely chopped

½ tsp chili powder

½ tsp light brown sugar

¾ pint/425 ml/2 cups water

juice of ½ lemon

salt

sliced scallions, to garnish

1 Cook the vegetables separately in a saucepan of salted boiling water for 4–5 minutes, drain well and chill.

2 To make the dressing, heat the oil in a frying skillet and fry the peanuts, tossing frequently, for 3–4 minutes.

3 Remove from the pan with a slotted spoon and drain on absorbent paper towels. Process the peanuts in a food processor or crush with a rolling pin until a fine mixture is formed.

4 Pour all but 1 tablespoon of the oil from the pan and fry the garlic and onion for 1 minute. Add the chili powder, sugar, a pinch of salt and the water and bring to the boil.

5 Stir in the peanuts. Reduce the heat and simmer for 4–5 minutes, until the sauce thickens. Add the lemon juice and set aside to cool.

6 Arrange the vegetables in a serving dish and spoon the peanut dressing into the center. Garnish and serve.

COOK'S TIP

Virgin olive oil, which has a fine aroma and flavor, is made by the cold pressing of olives. However, it may have a slightly higher acidity level than extra-virgin oil.

minted fennel salad

serves four

1 bulb fennel

lemon juice

2 small oranges

1 small or ½ a large cucumber

1 tbsp chopped mint

1 tbsp virgin olive oil

2 eggs, hard cooked

COOK'S TIP

Fennel will discolor if it is left
for any length of time without
a dressing. To prevent any
discoloration, place it in
a bowl of water and sprinkle
with lemon juice.

1 Using a sharp knife, trim the outer leaves from the fennel. Slice the fennel bulb thinly into a bowl of water and sprinkle with lemon juice (see Cook's Tip).

2 Grate the rind of the oranges over a bowl. Using a sharp knife, pare away the orange peel, then segment the orange by carefully slicing between each line of pith. Do this over the bowl in order to retain the juice.

3 Cut the cucumber into ½ inch rounds, and cut these into quarters. Add the cucumber and mint to the fennel and orange mixture.

4 Pour the olive oil over the fennel and cucumber salad and toss well.

5 Peel and quarter the eggs and use these to decorate the top of the salad. Serve at once.

Meat Salads

If your idea of a meat salad is a slice of ham, a tomato, and a couple of lettuce leaves, then you're in for a delightful surprise. There are recipes here that feature ham, chicken, turkey, duck, beef, bacon, and sausages also play a starring role. There are robust dishes for the confirmed carnivore, subtle mixtures for the sophisticated palate, and spicy salads for those who like the heat! From arugula to radishes and from pasta to peanuts the combinations of flavors, colors, and textures provide a feast for the eyes as well as the taste buds. If you favor the traditional, then try Chef's Salad (see page 50) or Roast Beef Salad (see page 79), but if your tastes are more adventurous, perhaps Thai Style Chicken Salad (see page 66) or Wild Rice & Bacon Salad (see page 58) will fit the bill.

melon, chorizo & artichoke salad

serves eight

serves eight

12 small globe artichokes

juice of ½ lemon

2 tbsp Spanish olive oil

1 small orange-fleshed melon, such
    as cantaloupe

7 oz/200 g chorizo sausage, outer
    casing removed

fresh tarragon or flatleaf parsley
    sprigs, to garnish

DRESSING

3 tbsp Spanish extra-virgin olive oil

1 tbsp red wine vinegar

1 tsp prepared mustard

1 tbsp chopped fresh tarragon

salt and pepper

COOK'S TIP

With your hands,
break off the toughest outer
leaves at the base until the
tender inside leaves are visible.
Using a pair of scissors,
cut the spiky tips off the leaves.
Using a sharp knife, pare the
dark green skin from the base
and down the stem.

---

1 Prepare the artichokes (see Cook's Tip) then brush the cut surfaces of the artichokes with lemon juice to prevent discoloration. Carefully remove the choke (the mass of silky hairs) by pulling it out with your fingers or by scooping it out with a spoon. It is very important to remove all the choke on older artichokes, as the little barbs, if eaten, can irritate the throat. Cut the artichokes into fourths and brush them again with lemon juice.

2 Heat the olive oil in a large, heavy-bottom skillet. Add the prepared artichokes and cook, stirring frequently, for 5 minutes, or until the artichoke leaves are golden brown. Remove from the skillet, then transfer to a large serving bowl and let cool.

3 To prepare the melon, cut in half and scoop out the seeds with a spoon. Cut the flesh into bite-size cubes. Add to the cooled artichokes. Cut the chorizo into bite-size chunks and add to the melon and artichokes.

4 To make the dressing, place all the ingredients in a small bowl and whisk together. Just before serving, pour the dressing over the prepared salad ingredients and toss together. Serve the salad garnished with tarragon or parsley sprigs.

chef's salad

serves six

- 1 iceberg lettuce, shredded
- 6 oz/175 g cooked ham, cut into thin strips
- 6 oz/175 g cooked tongue, cut into thin strips
- 12 oz/350 g cooked chicken, cut into thin strips
- 6 oz/175 g Swiss cheese
- 4 tomatoes, quartered
- 3 hard-cooked eggs, shelled and quartered
- 1¾ cups Thousand Island Dressing

1 Arrange the lettuce on a large serving platter. Arrange the cold meat decoratively on top.

2 Cut the Swiss cheese into thin sticks, sprinkle over the salad, and arrange the tomato and egg quarters round the edge of the platter.

3 Serve the salad immediately, handing the dressing separately.

1

2

3

VARIATION

To make a Cobb's Salad, substitute the Swiss cheese for Roquefort, and add an avocado, diced. Omit the tongue and replace the ham with crisp, cooked bacon, chopped. Use a Vinaigarette dressing to serve (see p7).

artichoke & prosciutto salad

serves four

9½ oz/275 g canned artichoke
    hearts in oil, drained

4 small tomatoes

1 oz/25 g sun-dried tomatoes in oil

1½ oz/40 g prosciutto

1 oz/25 g pitted black olives, halved

fresh basil leaves

DRESSING

3 tbsp olive oil

1 tbsp white wine vinegar

1 garlic clove, crushed

½ tsp mild mustard

1 tsp clear honey

salt and pepper

3 To make the dressing, place the olive oil, wine vinegar, garlic, mustard, honey, and salt and pepper to taste in a screw-top jar and shake vigorously until the ingredients are well blended.

4 Pour the dressing over the salad and toss together. Serve the salad garnished with a few whole basil leaves.

COOK'S TIP
Use bottled artichokes in oil if you can find them as they have a better flavor. If only canned artichokes are available, rinse them carefully to remove the salty liquid.

1 Make sure the artichoke hearts are thoroughly drained, then cut them into quarters and place in a bowl. Cut each fresh tomato into wedges. Slice the sun-dried tomatoes into thin strips. Cut the prosciutto into thin strips and add to the bowl with the tomatoes and olive halves.

2 Keeping a few basil leaves whole for garnishing, tear the remainder into small pieces and add to the bowl containing the other salad ingredients.

warm mushroom, spinach & pancetta salad

serves four

generous 6 cups fresh baby
  spinach leaves

2 tbsp olive oil

5½ oz/150 g pancetta cubetti

10 oz/280 g mixed wild
  mushrooms, sliced

DRESSING

5 tbsp olive oil

1 tbsp balsamic vinegar

1 tsp Dijon mustard

pinch of sugar

salt and pepper

1 To make the dressing, place the olive oil, vinegar, mustard, sugar, salt, and pepper in a small bowl and whisk together. Rinse the baby spinach under cold running water, then drain and place in a large salad bowl.

2 Heat the oil in a large skillet. Add the pancetta and cook for 3 minutes. Add the mushrooms and cook for 3–4 minutes, or until tender.

3 Pour the dressing into the skillet and immediately turn the cooked mixture and dressing into the bowl with the spinach. Toss until coated with the dressing and serve at once.

VARIATION

Try using wholegrain mustard
instead of the smoother Dijon
mustard to achieve an alternative
texture for the dressing.

walnut, pear & crispy bacon salad

serves four

4 lean bacon slices

generous ⅝ cup walnut halves

2 Red Bartlett pears, cored and
    sliced lengthwise

1 tbsp lemon juice

6 oz/175 g watercress, tough stalks
    removed

FOR THE DRESSING

3 tbsp extra-virgin olive oil

2 tbsp lemon juice

½ tsp honey

salt and pepper

COOK'S TIP

Snip the edges of
the bacon with scissors
before broiling to prevent
it curling while cooking.
This will make it easier to turn
each piece over, and then
to chop once cooked.

1 Preheat the broiler to high.
Arrange the bacon on a foil-lined broiler pan and cook under the preheated broiler until well browned and crisp. Let cool, then cut into ½-inch/1-cm pieces.

2 Meanwhile, heat a dry skillet over medium heat and lightly toast the walnuts, shaking the skillet frequently, for 3 minutes, or until lightly browned. Let cool.

3 Toss the pears in the lemon juice to prevent discoloration. Put the watercress, walnuts, pears, and bacon into a salad bowl.

4 To make the dressing, whisk the oil, lemon juice, and honey together in a small bowl or pitcher. Season to taste with salt and pepper, then pour over the salad. Toss well to combine and serve.

crispy spinach & bacon

serves four

4 tbsp olive oil

4 strips of lean bacon, diced

1 thick slice of white bread, crusts removed, cut into cubes

1 lb/450 g fresh spinach, torn or shredded

1 Heat 2 tablespoons of the olive oil over high heat in a large skillet. Add the diced bacon to the skillet and cook for 3–4 minutes, or until crisp. Remove with a slotted spoon, draining carefully, and set aside.

2 Toss the cubes of bread in the fat remaining in the skillet over high heat for about 4 minutes, or until crisp and golden. Remove the croutons with a slotted spoon, draining carefully, and set them aside.

3 Add the remaining oil to the skillet and heat. Toss the spinach in the oil over high heat for about 3 minutes, or until it has just wilted. Turn into a serving bowl and sprinkle with the bacon and croutons. Serve immediately.

COOK'S TIP

Use day-old bread rather than fresh bread as it will be slightly drier and will produce crispier croutons.

wild rice & bacon salad

serves four

generous ¾ cup wild rice

2½ cups water or more, if necessary

½ cup pecans or walnuts

2 tbsp vegetable oil

4 slices smoked bacon, diced or
    sliced

3–4 shallots, finely chopped

5 tbsp walnut oil

2–3 tbsp sherry or apple vinegar

2 tbsp chopped fresh dill

8–12 large scallops, cut in half
    lengthwise

salt and pepper

lemon and lime slices, to serve

1 Put the wild rice in a saucepan with the water and bring to a boil, stirring once or twice. Reduce the heat, cover, and simmer gently for 30–50 minutes, depending on whether you prefer a chewy or tender texture. Using a fork, fluff the rice into a large bowl and set aside to cool slightly.

2 Meanwhile, dry-fry the nuts in a skillet, stirring frequently, for 2–3 minutes until just beginning to color. Cool and chop coarsely, then set aside.

3 Heat 1 tbsp of the vegetable oil in the pan. Stir in the bacon and cook, stirring occasionally, until crisp and brown. Transfer to paper towels to drain. Remove some of the oil from the pan and stir in the shallots. Cook, stirring occasionally, for 3–4 minutes, until soft.

4 Stir the toasted nuts, bacon, and shallots into the rice. Add the walnut oil, vinegar, half the chopped dill, and salt and pepper to taste. Toss well to combine the ingredients, then set aside.

5 Brush a large nonstick skillet with the remaining oil. Heat until very hot, add the scallops and cook for 1 minute on each side until golden (do not overcook). Remove them from the skillet.

6 Divide the wild rice salad among 4 plates. Top with the scallops and sprinkle with the remaining dill. Garnish with a sprig of dill, if desired, and serve immediately with the lemon and lime slices.

potato & sausage salad

serves four

1 lb/450 g waxy potatoes

1 radicchio or lollo rosso lettuce

1 green bell pepper, sliced

6 oz/175 g Italian sausage, sliced

1 red onion, halved and sliced

4½ oz/125 g sun-dried tomatoes,
    sliced

2 tbsp shredded fresh basil

DRESSING

1 tbsp balsamic vinegar

1 tsp tomato paste

2 tbsp olive oil

salt and pepper

COOK'S TIP

Any sliced Italian sausage
or salami can be used in this
salad. Italy is home of the
salami and there are numerous
varieties to choose from. Those
from the south tend to be more
highly spiced than those from
the north of the country.

1 Cook the potatoes in a pan of
boiling water for 20 minutes or
until cooked through. Drain and let cool.

2 Line a large serving platter with the
radicchio or lollo rosso lettuce leaves.

3 Slice the cooled potatoes and
arrange them in layers on the
lettuce-lined serving platter together
with the sliced green bell pepper, sliced
Italian sausage, red onion, sun-dried
tomatoes, and shredded fresh basil.

4 In a small bowl, whisk the
balsamic vinegar, tomato paste,
and olive oil together and season to
taste with salt and pepper. Pour the
dressing over the potato salad and
serve immediately.

serrano ham & mushroom salad

serves four

½ small galia melon, peeled and
    sliced
12 very thin slices of Serrano ham,
    cut into strips
6 ripe fresh figs, trimmed and
    quartered
5½ oz/150 g mushrooms
1 avocado
3 tbsp lemon juice
4 tbsp olive oil
pepper
sprigs of fresh flatleaf parsley,
    to garnish

COOK'S TIP

Serrano ham makes an exquisite
snack and small amounts add
a delightful flavor to a wide
variety of dishes such as soups,
vegetables, or pasta.

1 Divide the melon slices, ham strips, and fig quarters between serving plates. Wipe the mushrooms clean with a damp, clean cloth, then slice them thickly and scatter them over the salad.

2 Using a knife, cut the avocado in half and remove the pit. Remove and discard the skin, and cut the flesh into slices. Brush the slices with 1 tablespoon of the lemon juice to prevent discoloration, then arrange them over the top of the salad.

3 In a separate bowl, pour in the remaining lemon juice and all the olive oil and stir until thoroughly mixed. Season with pepper. Pour the mixture over the salad, ensuring that all the salad ingredients are well coated. Garnish with sprigs of fresh parsley and serve.

turkey & rice salad

4 cups chicken stock

scant 1 cup mixed long-grain and wild rice

2 tbsp corn oil

8 oz/225 g skinless, boneless turkey breast, trimmed of all visible fat and cut into thin strips

2 cups snow peas

4 oz/115 g oyster mushrooms, torn into pieces

¼ cup shelled pistachio nuts, finely chopped

2 tbsp chopped fresh cilantro

1 tbsp snipped fresh garlic chives

salt and pepper

1 tbsp balsamic vinegar

fresh garlic chives, to garnish

1 Set aside 3 tablespoons of the chicken stock and bring the remainder to a boil in a large pan. Add the rice and cook for 30 minutes, or until tender. Drain and let cool slightly.

2 Meanwhile, heat 1 tablespoon of the oil in a preheated wok or skillet. Stir-fry the turkey over medium heat for 3–4 minutes, or until cooked through. Using a slotted spoon, transfer the turkey to a dish. Add the snow peas and mushrooms to the wok and stir-fry for 1 minute. Add the reserved stock, bring to a boil, then reduce the heat, cover, and let simmer for 3–4 minutes. Transfer the vegetables to the dish and let cool slightly.

3 Thoroughly mix the rice, turkey, snow peas, mushrooms, nuts, cilantro, and garlic chives together, then season to taste with salt and pepper. Drizzle with the remaining corn oil and the vinegar and garnish with fresh garlic chives. Serve warm.

VARIATION

This salad would also look spectacular made with red rice. Cook as in the main recipe or follow the package instructions.

belgian endive, orange & turkey salad

serves two

2 heads Belgian endive

2 oranges

scant ½ cup strips of cooked turkey

DRESSING

6 tbsp oil

3 tbsp orange juice

pinch of sugar

pinch of mustard powder

salt and pepper

1 Remove the outer leaves from the Belgian endive and slice them thinly widthwise. Peel the oranges and slice thinly against the grain, removing all the seeds.

2 Combine the Belgian endive and orange in a large mixing bowl.

3 To make the dressing, combine the oil, orange juice, sugar, mustard, salt, and pepper in a jar with a tight-fitting lid, then screw on the lid, and shake well. Pour the dressing over the Belgian endive and orange, toss well to blend, cover with plastic wrap, and chill for at least 1 hour.

COOK'S TIP

Reserve two or three pieces of orange before tossing the salad and then use to garnish.

4 Remove the salad from the refrigerator 10 minutes before serving. Toss once more, if desired, then arrange on attractive plates, and sprinkle the turkey strips on top.

warm chicken liver salad

serves four

salad greens

1 tbsp olive oil

1 small onion, chopped finely

1 lb/450 g frozen chicken livers, thawed

1 tsp chopped fresh tarragon

1 tsp wholegrain mustard

2 tbsp balsamic vinegar

salt and pepper

1 Arrange the salad greens on serving plates.

2 Heat the oil in a nonstick skillet, add the onion, and cook for 5 minutes, or until softened. Add the chicken livers, tarragon, and mustard and cook for 3–5 minutes, stirring, until tender. Put on top of the salad greens.

3 Add the vinegar, salt, and pepper to the skillet and heat, stirring constantly, until all the sediment has been lifted from the skillet. Pour the dressing over the chicken livers and serve warm.

COOK'S TIP

Make sure that you buy the freshest liver. If using frozen liver make sure that it smells fresh once thawed.

roast chicken salad with orange dressing

serves four

9 oz/250 g young spinach leaves

handful of fresh parsley leaves

½ cucumber, thinly sliced

¾ cup chopped walnuts, toasted

12 oz/350 g boneless lean roast
   chicken, thinly sliced

2 red apples

1 tbsp lemon juice

ORANGE DRESSING

2 tbsp extra-virgin olive oil

juice of 1 orange

finely grated rind of ½ orange

1 tbsp crème fraîche or sour cream

sprigs of fresh flatleaf parsley,
   to garnish

orange wedges, to serve

1 Wash and drain the spinach and parsley leaves, if necessary, then arrange on a large serving platter. Top with the cucumber and walnuts. Arrange the chicken slices over the salad.

2 Core the apples, then cut them in half. Cut each half into slices and brush with the lemon juice to prevent discoloration. Arrange the apple slices on top of the salad.

3 Put the dressing ingredients into a screw-top jar, screw on the lid tightly, and shake well until thoroughly combined. Drizzle the dressing over the salad, garnish with parsley sprigs, and serve with orange wedges.

thai-style chicken salad

serves four

14 oz/400 g small new potatoes,
    scrubbed and cut in half,
    lengthwise

7 oz/200 g baby corn cobs, sliced

1½ cups bean sprouts

3 scallions, trimmed and sliced

4 cooked, skinless chicken
    breasts, sliced

1 tbsp chopped lemongrass

2 tbsp chopped fresh cilantro

salt and pepper

DRESSING

6 tbsp chili oil or sesame oil

2 tbsp lime juice

1 tbsp light soy sauce

1 tbsp chopped fresh cilantro

1 small, red chili, seeded and
    finely chopped

GARNISH

wedges of lime

fresh cilantro leaves

1 Bring two pans of water to the boil. Put the potatoes into one pan and cook for 15 minutes until tender. Put the corn cobs into the other pan and cook for 5 minutes until tender. Drain the potatoes and corn cobs well and let cool.

2 When the vegetables are cool, transfer them into a large serving dish. Add the bean sprouts, scallions, chicken, lemongrass, and cilantro and season with salt and pepper.

3 To make the dressing, put all the ingredients into a screw-top jar and shake well. Alternatively, put them into a bowl and mix together well. Drizzle the dressing over the salad and garnish with lime wedges and cilantro leaves. Serve at once.

COOK'S TIP
For a healthy way to cook
the chicken, score the flesh and
then broil under a medium-high
heat for 10 minutes each side,
or until cooked through.

chicken, cheese & arugula salad

serves four

5½ oz/150 g arugula leaves

2 celery stalks, trimmed and sliced

½ cucumber, sliced

2 scallions, trimmed and sliced

2 tbsp chopped fresh parsley

1 oz/25 g walnut pieces

12 oz/350 g boneless roast
    chicken, sliced

4½ oz/125 g Stilton cheese, cubed

handful of seedless red grapes,
    cut in half (optional)

salt and pepper

DRESSING

2 tbsp olive oil

1 tbsp sherry vinegar

1 tsp Dijon mustard

1 tbsp chopped mixed herbs

1 Wash the arugula leaves, pat dry with paper towels, and put them into a large salad bowl. Add the celery, cucumber, scallions, parsley, and walnuts and mix together well. Transfer onto a large serving platter. Arrange the chicken slices over the salad, then scatter over the cheese. Add the red grapes, if using. Season well with salt and pepper.

2 To make the dressing, put all the ingredients into a screw-top jar and shake well. Alternatively, put them into a bowl and mix together well. Drizzle the dressing over the salad and serve.

VARIATION

If you can't obtain Stilton, or you want to try a ritzier version of this salad, replace with the equally tasty Roquefort cheese.

chicken pinwheels with blue cheese & herbs

serves four

2 tbsp pine nuts, lightly toasted

2 tbsp chopped fresh parsley

2 tbsp chopped fresh thyme

1 garlic clove, chopped

1 tbsp grated lemon zest

salt and pepper

4 large, skinless chicken breasts

9 oz/250 g blue cheese, such as
    Stilton, crumbled

GARNISH

twists of lemon

sprigs of fresh thyme

fresh green and red lettuce leaves,
    to serve

1 Put the pine nuts into a food processor with the parsley, thyme, garlic, and lemon zest. Season with salt and pepper.

2 Pound the chicken breasts lightly to flatten them. Spread them on one side with the pine nut mixture, then top with the cheese. Roll them up from one short end to the other, so that the filling is enclosed. Wrap the rolls individually in aluminum foil, and seal well. Transfer into a steamer, or a metal colander placed over a pan of boiling water, cover tightly, and steam for 10–12 minutes, or until cooked through.

3 Arrange the lettuce leaves on a large serving platter. Remove the chicken from the heat, discard the foil, and cut the chicken rolls into slices. Arrange the slices over the lettuce leaves, garnish with twists of lemon and sprigs of thyme, and serve.

VARIATION

This recipe could be used
as a main course for
a dinner party with an
accompaniment such as
a rice-based side dish.

layered chicken salad

serves four

1 lb10 oz/750 g new potatoes,
   scrubbed
1 red bell pepper, halved and
   deseeded
1 green bell pepper, halved and
   deseeded
2 small zucchini, sliced
1 small onion, thinly sliced
3 tomatoes, sliced
12 oz/350 g cooked chicken, sliced
chopped fresh chives, to garnish
YOGURT DRESSING
²⁄₃ cup lowfat plain yogurt
3 tbsp lowfat mayonnaise
1 tbsp chopped fresh chives
salt and pepper

1 Put the potatoes into a large pan, add just enough cold water to cover, and bring to a boil. Lower the heat, cover, and simmer for 15–20 minutes until tender.

2 Meanwhile, place the bell pepper halves, skin side up, under a preheated hot broiler and broil until the skins blacken and begin to char.

3 Remove the bell peppers with tongs, place in a bowl, and cover with plastic wrap. Set aside until cool enough to handle, then peel off the skins, and slice the flesh.

4 Bring a small pan of lightly salted water to a boil. Add the zucchini, bring back to a boil, and simmer for 3 minutes. Drain, rinse under cold running water to prevent any further cooking, and drain again. Set aside.

5 To make the dressing, whisk the yogurt, lowfat mayonnaise, and chopped chives together in a small bowl until well blended. Season to taste with salt and pepper.

6 When the potatoes are tender, drain, cool, and slice them. Add them to the dressing and mix gently to coat evenly. Spoon the potatoes onto 4 serving plates, dividing them equally.

7 Top each plate with one quarter of the bell pepper slices and zucchini. Layer one quarter of the onion and tomato slices, then the sliced chicken, on top of each serving. Garnish with chopped chives and serve immediately.

spinach salad

serves four

½ cup mushrooms

3½ oz/100 g baby spinach, washed

3 oz/85 g radicchio leaves, shredded

3½ oz/100 g cooked skinless
    chicken breast fillet

2 oz/55 g prosciutto

2 tbsp olive oil

finely grated rind of ½ orange and
    juice of 1 orange

1 tbsp plain yogurt

salt and pepper

1 Wipe the mushrooms with a damp cloth or damp paper towels to remove any dirt.

2 Mix together the spinach and radicchio in a large salad bowl.

3 Using a sharp knife, thinly slice the mushrooms and add them to the salad bowl.

4 Shred the cooked chicken breast with your fingers and tear the prosciutto into strips. Mix them into the salad.

5 To make the dressing, place the olive oil, grated orange rind, orange juice, and yogurt into a screw-top jar. Shake the jar vigorously until the mixture is thoroughly combined. Season to taste with salt and pepper.

6 Drizzle the dressing over the spinach salad and toss to mix well. Serve.

VARIATION

Spinach is delicious when served raw. Try raw spinach in a salad garnished with bacon or garlicky croutons. The young leaves have a wonderfully sharp flavor.

waldorf summer chicken salad

serves four

1 lb 2 oz red dessert apples, diced

3 tbsp fresh lemon juice

⅔ cup light mayonnaise

1 head of celery

4 shallots, sliced

1 garlic clove, finely chopped

¾ cup walnuts, chopped

1 lb 2 oz cooked chicken, cubed

1 Cos lettuce

pepper

sliced apple and walnuts, to garnish

VARIATION

Instead of the shallots,
use scallions for a milder
flavor. Trim the scallions
and slice finely.

1 Place the apples in a bowl with the lemon juice and 1 tablespoon of mayonnaise. Leave for 40 minutes.

2 Using a sharp knife, slice the celery very thinly.

3 Add the celery, shallots, garlic, and walnuts to the apple and mix together.

4 Stir in the mayonnaise and blend thoroughly.

5 Add the cooked chicken to the bowl and mix well.

6 Line a glass salad bowl or serving dish with the lettuce leaves. Pile the chicken salad into the center, sprinkle with pepper, and garnish with the apple slices and walnuts.

COOK'S TIP

Soaking the apples
in lemon juice prevents
discoloration.

hot & sour beef salad

serves four

1 tsp black peppercorns

1 tsp coriander seeds

1 dried red bird-eye chili

¼ tsp Chinese five-spice powder

9 oz/250 g beef tenderloin

1 tbsp dark soy sauce

6 scallions

1 carrot

¼ cucumber

8 radishes

1 red onion

¼ head Napa cabbage

2 tbsp peanut oil

1 garlic clove, crushed

1 tsp finely chopped lemongrass

1 tbsp chopped fresh mint

1 tbsp chopped fresh cilantro

DRESSING

3 tbsp lime juice

1 tbsp light soy sauce

2 tsp soft light brown sugar

1 tsp sesame oil

1 Crush the peppercorns, coriander seeds, and chili in a mortar with a pestle, then mix with the five-spice powder, and sprinkle on a plate. Brush the beef all over with soy sauce, then roll it in the spices to coat evenly.

2 Cut the scallions into 2½ inch/ 6 cm lengths, then shred finely lengthwise. Place in ice water until curled. Drain well.

3 Trim the carrot and cut into very thin diagonal slices. Halve the cucumber, scoop out and discard the seeds, then slice the flesh thinly. Trim the radishes and cut into flower shapes.

4 Slice the onion thinly. Roughly shred the Napa cabbage leaves. Toss all the vegetables together in a large salad bowl.

VARIATION
You can control the heat of this dish by altering the amount of lemongrass and chili seeds used.

5 Heat the oil in a skillet and fry the garlic and lemongrass until golden. Add the beef and cook for 3–4 minutes, turning once. Remove from the heat.

6 Slice the beef thinly and toss into the salad with the mint and cilantro. Mix together the dressing ingredients and stir into the skillet, then spoon over the salad. Serve immediately.

rare beef pasta salad

serves four

1 lb/450 g round or sirloin steak in
   a single piece

4 cups dried fusilli

4 tbsp olive oil

2 tbsp lime juice

2 tbsp Thai fish sauce (see Cook's Tip)

2 tsp honey

4 scallions, sliced

1 cucumber, peeled and cut into
   1 inch/2.5 cm chunks

3 tomatoes, cut into wedges

1 tbsp finely chopped fresh mint

salt and pepper

2 Meanwhile, bring a large pan of
   lightly salted water to a boil. Add
the pasta, bring back to a boil, and
cook for 8–10 minutes or until tender,
but still firm to the bite. Drain the
fusilli, refresh in cold water, and drain
again thoroughly. Toss the fusilli in the
olive oil and set aside until required.

3 Combine the lime juice, fish sauce,
   and honey in a small pan and
cook over medium heat for 2 minutes.

4 Add the scallions, cucumber,
   tomatoes, and mint to the pan,
then add the steak and mix well.
Season to taste with salt.

5 Transfer the fusilli to a large,
   warm serving dish and top with
the steak and salad mixture. Serve just
warm or let cool completely.

1 Season the steak with salt and
   pepper. Broil or pan-fry it for
4 minutes on each side. Let rest for 5
minutes, then slice thinly across the grain.

COOK'S TIP

Thai fish sauce, also known as
nam pla, is made from salted
anchovies and has quite a strong
flavor, so it should be used with
discretion. It is available from
some supermarkets
and from Asian food stores.

roast beef salad

serves four

1 lb10 oz/750 g beef fillet, trimmed
    of any visible fat

pepper

2 tsp Worcestershire sauce

3 tbsp olive oil

14 oz/400 g green beans

3½ oz/100 g small pasta, such as
    orecchiette

2 red onions, finely sliced

1 large head radicchio

generous ¼ cup green olives, pitted

scant ⅓ cup shelled hazelnuts, whole

FOR THE DRESSING

1 tsp Dijon mustard

2 tbsp white wine vinegar

5 tbsp olive oil

1 Preheat the oven to 425°F/220°C.
Rub the beef with pepper to taste
and Worcestershire sauce. Heat 2
tablespoons of the oil in a small
roasting pan over high heat, add the
beef, and sear on all sides. Transfer the
dish to the preheated oven and roast
for 30 minutes. Remove and let cool.

2 Bring a large pan of water to a
boil, add the beans, and cook for
5 minutes, or until just tender. Remove
with a slotted spoon and refresh the
beans under cold running water. Drain
and put into a large bowl.

3 Return the bean cooking water to
a boil, add the pasta, and cook
for 11 minutes, or until tender. Drain,
return to the pan, and toss with the
remaining oil.

4 Add the pasta to the beans with
the onions, radicchio leaves,
olives, and hazelnuts in a serving dish
or salad bowl and arrange some thinly
sliced beef on top.

5 Whisk the dressing ingredients
together in a separate bowl, then
pour over the salad and serve at once
with extra sliced beef.

beef & peanut salad

serves four

½ head Napa cabbage
1 large carrot
4 oz/115 g radishes
3½ oz/100 g baby corn cobs
1 tbsp peanut oil
1 red chili, seeded and finely
   chopped
1 clove garlic, finely chopped
   12 oz/350 g lean beef (such as
   fillet, sirloin or rump), trimmed
   and shredded finely 1 tbsp dark
   soy sauce
¼ cup fresh peanuts, optional
sliced red chili, to garnish
DRESSING
1 tbsp smooth peanut butter
1 tsp superfine sugar
2 tbsp light soy sauce
1 tbsp sherry vinegar
salt and pepper

1 Finely shred the Napa cabbage and arrange attractively on a platter.

2 Peel the carrot and cut into very thin strips. Wash, trim, and quarter the radishes, and halve the baby corn lengthwise. Arrange these ingredients around the edge of the dish and set aside.

3 Heat the peanut oil in a non-stick wok or large skillet until really hot.

4 Add the red chili, garlic, and beef to the wok or skillet and cook for 5 minutes.

5 Add the dark soy sauce and cook for a further 1-2 minutes until tender and cooked through.

COOK'S TIP

If preferred, use chicken, turkey, lean pork, or even strips of venison instead of beef in this recipe. Cut off all visible fat before you begin.

6 Meanwhile, make the dressing. Place all of the ingredients in a small bowl and blend them together until smooth.

7 Place the hot cooked beef in the center of the salad ingredients. Spoon over the dressing and sprinkle with a few peanuts, if using. Garnish with slices of red chili and serve immediately.

chili beef stir-fry salad

serves four

1 lb/450 g lean rump steak

2 cloves garlic, crushed

1 tsp chili powder

½ tsp salt

1 tsp ground coriander

1 ripe avocado

2 tbsp sunflower oil

15 oz/425 g canned red kidney beans

6 oz/175 g cherry tomatoes, halved

1 large packet tortilla chips

shredded Iceberg lettuce

chopped fresh cilantro, to serve

1 Using a sharp knife, slice the beef into thin strips.

2 Place the garlic, chili powder, salt, and ground cilantro in a large bowl and mix until well combined.

3 Add the strips of beef to the marinade and toss well to coat all over.

4 Using a sharp knife, peel the avocado. Slice the avocado lengthwise and then crosswise to form small dice.

5 Heat the oil in a large preheated wok. Add the beef and cook for 5 minutes, tossing frequently.

6 Add the kidney beans, tomatoes, and avocado, and heat through for 2 minutes.

7 Arrange a bed of tortilla chips and Iceberg lettuce around the edge of a large serving plate and spoon the beef mixture into the center. Alternatively, serve the tortilla chips and Iceberg lettuce separately.

8 Garnish with chopped fresh cilantro and serve immediately.

grilled beef salad

serves four

DRESSING

2 tbsp sesame oil

2 tbsp fish sauce

2 tbsp sweet sherry

2 tbsp oyster sauce

1 tbsp lime juice

1 fresh red chili, seeded and
chopped finely

scant ⅔ cup dried oyster mushrooms

1 lb 5 oz/600 g rump steak

1 red bell pepper, seeded and
sliced thinly

generous ¼ cup roasted cashew nuts

red and green lettuce leaves,
to serve

mint leaves, to garnish

COOK'S TIP

If you have time,
leave the beef to marinate
in the dressing for up
to 30 minutes to absorb
the flavors.

---

1 Slice the peppers thinly. To make the dressing, place the sesame oil, fish sauce, sherry, oyster sauce, lime juice, and chili in a bowl and whisk to combine.

2 Place the mushrooms in a bowl, then cover with boiling water and let stand for 20 minutes. Drain and cut into thin slices.

3 Grill the beef, either on a ridged iron grill pan or under the broiler, turning once, for 5 minutes, or until browned on both sides and rare in the middle, or cook longer if desired.

4 Slice the steak into thin strips and place in a bowl with the mushrooms, bell pepper, and nuts. Add the dressing and toss together.

5 Arrange the lettuce on a serving platter and place the beef mixture on top. Garnish with mint and serve at room temperature.

duck & radish salad

serves four

12 oz boneless duck breasts,
  skinned
2 tbsp all-purpose flour
1 egg
2 tbsp water
2 tbsp sesame seeds
3 tbsp sesame oil
½ head Chinese cabbage, shredded
3 celery stalks, sliced finely
8 radishes, trimmed and halved
salt and pepper
fresh basil leaves, to garnish
DRESSING
finely grated peel of 1 lime
2 tbsp lime juice
2 tbsp olive oil
1 tbsp light soy sauce
1 tbsp chopped fresh basil

1 Put each duck breast between sheets of baking parchment or plastic wrap. Use a meat mallet or rolling pin to beat them out and flatten them slightly.

2 Sprinkle the flour onto a large plate and season with salt and pepper.

3 Beat the egg and water together in a shallow bowl, then sprinkle the sesame seeds onto a separate plate.

4 Dip the duck breasts first into the seasoned flour, then into the egg mixture and finally into the sesame seeds, to coat the duck evenly.

5 Heat the sesame oil in a preheated wok or large skillet.

6 Fry the duck breasts over a medium heat for about 8 minutes, turning once. To test whether they are cooked, insert a sharp knife into the thickest part – the juices should run clear. Lift them out and drain on paper towels.

7 To make the dressing for the salad, whisk together the lime peel and juice, olive oil, soy sauce, and chopped basil. Season with a little salt and pepper.

8 Arrange the Chinese cabbage, celery, and radish on a serving plate. Slice the duck breasts thinly and place on top of the salad.

9 Drizzle with the dressing and garnish with fresh basil leaves. Serve at once.

roast duck salad

serves four

2 duck breasts

2 Boston lettuces, shredded

1 cup bean sprouts

1 yellow bell pepper, seeded and
   cut into thin strips

½ cucumber, seeded and cut into
   short thin sticks

GARNISH

2 tsp shredded lime zest

2 tbsp shredded coconut, toasted

DRESSING

juice of 2 limes

3 tbsp fish sauce

1 tbsp soft brown sugar

2 tsp sweet chili sauce

1 inch/2.5 cm fresh gingerroot,
   grated finely

3 tbsp chopped fresh mint

3 tbsp chopped fresh basil

1 Preheat the oven to 400°F/200°C.
Place the duck breasts on a rack
set over a roasting pan and roast in the
oven for 20–30 minutes, or until cooked
as desired and the skin is crisp. Remove
from the oven and set aside to cool.

2 In a large bowl, combine the
lettuce, bean sprouts, bell pepper
and cucumber. Cut the cooled duck into
strips and add to the salad. Mix well.

3 In a bowl, whisk together the
lime juice, fish sauce, sugar, chili
sauce, ginger, mint, and basil. Add the
dressing to the salad and toss well.

4 Turn the salad out onto a serving
platter and garnish with the lime
zest and shredded coconut before serving.

COOK'S TIP

Before adding the duck to the
preheated hot wok, swirl
the corn oil gently and carefully so
that it coats the sides as well as the
bottom of the wok.

Fish & Seafood

It is a curious fact that many people who dislike
hot fish dishes love seafood salads, and they
will cheerily tuck into a colorful Salade Niçoise

when they wouldn't dream of eating a tuna steak. Of course, this chapter is

even more of a joy for devoted fish lovers, offering such delights as Shrimp &

Mango Salad (see page 92), Seafood & Spinach Salad (see page 118), and the

ever-popular Caesar Salad (see page 122). There are easy, inexpensive salads

for family meals, based around canned tuna or smoked haddock, as well as

special occasion salads with more luxurious ingredients such as smoked

salmon and lobster. Perhaps the appeal of salads made with fish and seafood

is that they combine so well with a huge number of other ingredients, from

vegetables to fruit and from lentils to eggs.

smoked salmon & arugula salad

serves four

1¾ oz/50 g fresh arugula

1 tbsp chopped fresh flatleaf parsley

2 scallions, finely diced

2 large avocados

1 tbsp lemon juice

9 oz/250 g smoked salmon slices

LIME MAYONNAISE

½ cup mayonnaise

2 tbsp lime juice

finely grated rind of 1 lime

1 tbsp chopped fresh flatleaf parsley

sprigs of fresh flatleaf parsley,
    to garnish

lime wedges, to serve

COOK'S TIP

Arugula is a "super" food
and contains more vitamin C
than any other salad green.

1 Wash and drain the arugula, if necessary. Shred the leaves and arrange in 4 individual salad bowls or on 4 small plates. Top with the chopped parsley and scallions.

2 Halve, peel, and pit the avocados and cut into thin slices or small chunks. Brush with the lemon juice to prevent discoloration, then divide between the salad bowls. Mix together gently. Cut the smoked salmon into strips and scatter over the top.

3 Put the mayonnaise into a bowl, then add the lime juice and rind and the chopped parsley. Mix together well. Spoon some of the lime mayonnaise on top of each salad, garnish with parsley sprigs, and serve with lime wedges.

salmon & avocado salad

serves four

1 lb/450 g new potatoes

4 salmon steaks, about 4 oz/
115 g each

1 avocado

juice of ½ lemon

1¼ cups baby spinach leaves

4½ oz/125 g mixed small salad
greens, including watercress

12 cherry tomatoes, halved

scant ½ cup chopped walnuts

FOR THE DRESSING

3 tbsp unsweetened clear
apple juice

1 tsp balsamic vinegar

freshly ground black pepper

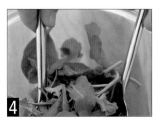

6 To make the dressing, mix the apple juice and vinegar together in a small bowl or pitcher and season well with pepper. Drizzle over the salads and serve at once.

1 Cut the new potatoes into bite-size pieces, put into a pan, and cover with cold water. Bring to a boil, then reduce the heat, cover, and let simmer for 10–15 minutes, or until just tender. Drain and keep warm.

2 Meanwhile, preheat the broiler to medium. Cook the salmon steaks under the preheated broiler for 10–15 minutes, depending on the thickness of the steaks, turning halfway through cooking. Remove from the broiler and keep warm.

3 While the potatoes and salmon are cooking, cut the avocado in half, remove and discard the pit, and peel the flesh. Cut the avocado flesh into slices and coat in the lemon juice to prevent it discoloring.

4 Toss the spinach leaves and mixed salad greens together in a large serving bowl until combined. Arrange 6 cherry tomato halves on each plate of salad.

5 Remove and discard the skin and any bones from the salmon. Flake the salmon and divide between the plates along with the potatoes. Sprinkle the walnuts over the salads.

tomato, salmon & shrimp salad

serves four

4 oz/115 g cherry or baby plum
   tomatoes

several lettuce leaves

4 ripe tomatoes, coarsely chopped

4½ oz/125 g smoked salmon

7 oz/200 g large cooked shrimp,
   thawed if frozen

1 tbsp Dijon mustard

2 tsp superfine sugar

2 tsp red wine vinegar

2 tbsp medium olive oil

few fresh dill sprigs

pepper

warmed rolls or ciabatta bread,
   to serve

1 Halve most of the cherry tomatoes. Place the lettuce leaves round the edge of a shallow bowl and add all the tomatoes and cherry tomatoes. Using scissors, snip the smoked salmon into strips and sprinkle over the tomatoes, then add the shrimp.

COOK'S TIP

This dish is designed to be quite casual, so when serving aim to scatter the ingredients, rather than arrange them.

2 Mix the mustard, sugar, vinegar, and oil together in a small bowl, then tear most of the dill sprigs into it. Mix well and pour over the salad. Toss well to coat the salad with the dressing. Snip the remaining dill over the top and season to taste with pepper.

3 Serve the salad with warmed rolls or ciabatta bread.

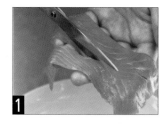

shrimp & mango salad

serves four

2 mangoes

2 cups peeled, cooked shrimp

DRESSING

juice from the mangoes

6 tbsp lowfat plain yogurt

2 tbsp reduced-calorie mayonnaise

1 tbsp lemon juice

salt and pepper

4 whole cooked shrimp, to garnish

salad greens, to serve

VARIATION

Add a dash or two of Tabasco sauce to the dressing to give it a spicy kick.

1 Cutting close to the pit, cut a large slice from one side of each mango, then cut another slice from the opposite side. Without breaking the skin, cut the flesh in the segments into squares, then push the skin inside out to expose the cubes, and cut away from the skin. Use a sharp knife to peel the remaining center section and cut the flesh away from the pit into cubes. Reserve any juice in a bowl and put the mango flesh in a separate bowl.

2 Add the shrimp to the mango flesh. Add the yogurt, mayonnaise, lemon juice, salt, and pepper to the juice and blend together.

3 Arrange the salad greens on a serving dish and add the mango flesh and shrimp. Pour the dressing over them and serve garnished with the whole shrimp.

russian salad

serves four

4 oz/115 g new potatoes

generous 1 cup frozen or shelled
　　fresh fava beans

4 oz/115 g baby carrots

4 oz/115 g baby corn

4 oz/115 g baby turnips

4 oz/115 g white mushrooms,
　　cut into thin sticks

12 oz/350 g cooked shelled
　　shrimp, deveined

½ cup mayonnaise

1 tbsp lemon juice

2 tbsp bottled capers, drained
　　and rinsed

salt and pepper

2 tbsp extra-virgin olive oil

2 hard-cooked eggs, shelled
　　and halved

4 canned anchovy fillets, drained
　　and halved

paprika, to garnish

1 Cook the new potatoes, fava beans, carrots, corn, and turnips simultaneously. Cook the potatoes in a large, heavy-bottom pan of lightly salted boiling water for 20 minutes. Cook the fava beans in a small pan of lightly salted water for 3 minutes, then drain, refresh under cold running water and set aside until required. Cook the carrots, corn, and turnips in a large, heavy-bottom pan of lightly salted boiling water for 6 minutes.

2 Mix the mushrooms and shrimp together in a bowl. Mix the mayonnaise and lemon juice together in a separate bowl, then fold half the mixture into the shrimp mixture. Fold in the capers and season to taste with salt and pepper.

3 Drain the mixed vegetables, refresh under cold running water and tip into a bowl. When the potatoes are cooked, drain, refresh under cold running water and tip into the bowl. Pop the fava beans out of their skins by pinching them between your index finger and thumb and add to the bowl. Add the olive oil and toss to coat. Divide the potatoes and vegetables between serving plates and top with the shrimp mixture. Place a hard-cooked egg half in the center of each and decorate with the halved anchovies. Dust the eggs with paprika and serve with the remaining mayonnaise mixture.

shrimp salad & toasted rice

serves four

8 oz/225 g peeled cooked shrimp,
 with tail shells left on
cayenne pepper
1 tbsp long grain rice
2 tbsp sunflower oil
1 large head Romaine lettuce with
 outer leaves removed or 2 hearts
½ small cucumber, peeled,
 deseeded and thinly sliced
1 small bunch chives, sliced into
 1 inch/2.5 cm pieces
handful of fresh mint leaves
salt and pepper
DRESSING
¼ cup rice vinegar
1 fresh red chili, deseeded and
 thinly sliced
3 inch/7.5 cm piece of lemongrass
 stalk, crushed
juice of 1 lime
2 tbsp Thai fish sauce
1 tsp sugar

1 Split each shrimp in half lengthwise, leaving the tail attached to one half. Remove the dark intestinal veins and pat dry on paper towels. Sprinkle with a little salt and cayenne pepper.

2 To make the dressing, combine the vinegar with the chili and lemongrass. Set aside to marinate.

3 Heat a wok or heavy skillet over high heat. Add the rice and stir until brown and fragrant. Turn into a mortar and cool completely. Crush gently with a pestle until coarse crumbs form.

4 Heat the oil in a clean pan and stir-fry the shrimp for 1 minute. Transfer to a plate and season with pepper.

5 Tear or shred the lettuce into bite-size pieces and transfer to a shallow salad bowl. Add the cucumber, chives, and mint leaves and toss to combine.

6 Remove the lemongrass and most of the chili slices from the rice vinegar and whisk in the lime juice, fish sauce, and sugar. Pour most of the dressing over the salad and toss well to mix. Top with the shrimp and drizzle with the remaining dressing. Sprinkle with the toasted rice and serve immediately.

thai noodle salad

serves four

1 oz/25 g dried wood ears

2 oz/55 g dried Chinese mushrooms

4 oz/115 g cellophane noodles

½ cup cooked lean ground pork

4 oz/115 g shelled raw shrimp

5 fresh red chilies, seeded and
  thinly sliced

1 tbsp chopped fresh cilantro

3 tbsp Thai fish sauce (nam pla)

3 tbsp lime juice

1 tbsp brown sugar

VARIATION

For extra flavor, use the strained
soaking water from the
mushrooms—not the wood
ears—for cooking the shrimp
and the cooked ground pork.

---

1 Put the wood ears and Chinese mushrooms in separate bowls and pour over enough boiling water to cover. Let soak for 30 minutes. After 20 minutes, put the cellophane noodles in a separate bowl and pour over enough hot water to cover. Let the noodles soak for 10 minutes, or according to the package instructions.

2 Drain the wood ears, rinse thoroughly and cut into small pieces. Drain the mushrooms, squeezing out as much liquid as possible. Cut off and discard the stalks and cut the caps in half. Pour just enough water into a pan to cover the bottom and bring to a boil. Add the pork, shrimp, wood ears, and mushrooms and let simmer, stirring, for 3 minutes, or until cooked through. Drain well. Drain the noodles and cut them into short lengths with scissors.

3 Put the chilies, cilantro, fish sauce, lime juice, and brown sugar in a salad bowl and stir until the sugar has dissolved. Add the noodles and shrimp and pork mixture, toss well, and serve.

coconut shrimp with cucumber salad

serves four

1 cup brown basmati rice

½ tsp coriander seeds

2 egg whites, lightly beaten

generous ¾ cup dry unsweetened
    coconut

24 raw jumbo shrimp, shelled and
    tails left intact

½ cucumber

4 scallions, thinly sliced lengthwise

1 tsp sesame oil

1 tbsp finely chopped fresh cilantro

1 lime, cut into wedges, to garnish

1 Bring a large pan of water to a boil, add the rice, and cook for 25 minutes, or until tender. Drain and keep in a strainer covered with a clean dish towel to absorb the steam.

COOK'S TIP

If you are using wooden skewers instead of metal ones, make sure you soak them thoroughly to stop them burning.

2 Meanwhile, soak 8 wooden skewers in cold water for 30 minutes, then drain.

3 Crush the coriander seeds in a mortar with a pestle. Heat a nonstick skillet over medium heat, add the crushed coriander seeds, and cook, turning, until they start to color. Tip onto a plate and set aside.

4 Put the egg whites into a shallow bowl and the coconut into a separate bowl. Roll each shrimp first in the egg whites, then in the coconut. Thread onto a skewer. Repeat so that each skewer is threaded with 3 coated shrimp.

5 Preheat the broiler to high. Using a potato peeler, peel long strips from the cucumber to create ribbons, put into a strainer to drain, then toss with the scallions and oil in a bowl, and set aside.

6 Cook the shrimp under the preheated broiler for 3–4 minutes on each side, or until pink and slightly browned.

7 Meanwhile, mix the rice with the toasted coriander seeds and fresh cilantro and press into 4 dariole molds or individual ramekins. Invert each mold onto a serving plate and divide the cucumber salad between the plates. Serve with the hot shrimp skewers, garnished with lime wedges.

tuna & fresh vegetable salad

DRESSING

4 tbsp reduced-calorie mayonnaise

4 tbsp lowfat plain yogurt

2 tbsp white wine vinegar

salt and pepper

12 cherry tomatoes, halved

1½ cups whole green beans,
    cut into 1 inch/2.5 cm pieces

8 oz/225 g zucchini, sliced thinly

3¼ cups thinly sliced
    white mushrooms

12 oz/350 g canned tuna in brine,
    drained and flaked

chopped fresh parsley, to garnish

salad greens, to serve

1 To make the dressing, put the mayonnaise, yogurt, vinegar, salt, and pepper in a screw-topped jar and shake together until the ingredients are well blended.

2 Put the tomatoes, beans, zucchini, and mushrooms in a bowl. Pour over the dressing and marinate for about 1 hour. Drain the tuna and flake in a separate bowl.

3 To serve, arrange the salad greens on a serving dish. Add the vegetables and then the tuna, and garnish with chopped parsley.

COOK'S TIP

To give a professional finish try to slice the mushrooms and zucchini to the same thickness.

salade niçoise

serves four

2 eggs

12 small new potatoes

salt

4 oz/115 g green beans

2 Romaine lettuces or

   3 Boston lettuces

7 oz/200 g canned tuna in oil

6 canned anchovy fillets

4 tomatoes

4 scallions

12 black olives

2 tbsp bottled capers, drained

2 tbsp pine nuts

DRESSING

6 tbsp extra-virgin olive oil

2 tbsp tarragon white wine vinegar

1 tsp Dijon mustard

1 garlic clove, finely chopped

1 Cook the eggs, potatoes, and beans simultaneously. Place the eggs in a pan and cover with cold water. Bring to a boil, then reduce the heat and boil gently for 12 minutes. Cook the potatoes in a pan of lightly salted boiling water for 12–15 minutes, or until tender, and cook the green beans in a separate pan of lightly salted boiling water for 3–5 minutes.

2 Meanwhile, prepare all the remaining ingredients. Coarsely chop the lettuces, drain and flake the tuna, then drain the anchovies and halve them lengthwise. Chop the tomatoes and slice the scallions. To make the dressing, place all the ingredients in a large salad bowl and beat well to mix.

3 Drain the beans and refresh in cold water. Add to the salad bowl with the lettuces, tuna, anchovies, tomatoes, scallions, olives, and capers. Drain the eggs, cool under cold running water and set aside. Drain the potatoes and add to the salad. Lightly toast the pine nuts in a dry skillet, shaking the skillet frequently, for 1–2 minutes, or until golden. Sprinkle them over the salad. Shell and chop the eggs and add them to the salad.

4 Whisk the dressing again, add it to the salad, toss to coat, and serve.

warm tuna & kidney bean salad

serves four

4 fresh tuna steaks, about
   6 oz/175 g each

1 tbsp olive oil

7 oz/200 g canned kidney beans

3½ oz/100 g canned corn kernels

2 scallions, trimmed and
   thinly sliced

DRESSING

5 tbsp extra-virgin olive oil

3 tbsp balsamic vinegar

1 tbsp lime juice

1 garlic clove, chopped

1 tbsp chopped fresh cilantro

salt and pepper

GARNISH

sprigs of fresh cilantro

wedges of lime

1 Preheat a heavy, ridged grill pan. While the pan is heating, brush the tuna steaks with olive oil, then season with salt and pepper. Cook the steaks for 2 minutes, then turn them over and cook on the other side for another 2 minutes, or according to your taste, but do not overcook. Remove from the heat and let cool slightly.

2 While the tuna is cooling, heat the kidney beans and corn according to the instructions on the cans, then drain.

3 To make the dressing, put all the ingredients into a small bowl and stir together well.

4 Put the kidney beans, corn, and scallions into a large bowl, pour over half of the dressing and mix together well. Divide the bean and corn salad between individual serving plates, then place a tuna steak on each one. Drizzle over the remaining dressing, garnish with sprigs of fresh cilantro and wedges of lime, and serve.

lentil & tuna salad

serves four

2 ripe tomatoes

1 small red onion

3 tbsp virgin olive oil

1 tbsp lemon juice

1 tsp whole-grain mustard

1 garlic clove, crushed

½ tsp ground cumin

½ tsp ground coriander

14 oz/400 g can lentils, drained

6½ oz/185 g can tuna, drained

2 tbsp chopped fresh cilantro

pepper

1 Using a sharp knife, deseed the tomatoes and then chop them into fine dice. Finely chop the red onion.

2 To make the dressing, whisk together the virgin olive oil, lemon juice, mustard, garlic, cumin, and ground coriander in a small bowl until thoroughly combined. Set aside until required.

3 Mix together the chopped onion, diced tomatoes, and drained lentils in a large bowl.

4 Flake the tuna with a fork and stir it into the onion, tomato, and lentil mixture. Stir in the chopped fresh cilantro and mix well.

5 Pour the dressing over the lentil and tuna salad and season with pepper to taste. Serve immediately.

COOK'S TIP

Lentils are an excellent source of protein and contain several important vitamins and minerals. Buy them dried for soaking and cooking yourself, or buy canned varieties for speed and convenience.

stuffed tomato salad

makes four

about 1½ oz cucumber, finely diced

3 large eggs

4 extra-large tomatoes, about
 10½ oz each

5 scallions, trimmed and diced

12 oz can tuna in olive oil, drained

1–2 tbsp mayonnaise

squeeze of lemon juice

small handful of basil leaves,
 plus extra for garnishing

salt and pepper

1 Put the cucumber in a plastic strainer, sprinkle with salt, and drain for 30 minutes.

2 Meanwhile, bring a pan of water to a boil, add the eggs, and cook for 12 minutes. Drain and place under running cold water to stop the cooking process.

3 Shell the eggs and chop the yolks and whites separately. Rinse the cucumber and pat dry with paper towels.

4 Working with one tomato at a time, slice off the top and use a small spoon to scoop out the insides;

reserve the insides. Drain the tomatoes upside-down on paper towels. Chop the reserved scooped-out insides and drain.

5 Put the chopped tomato in a bowl and add the chopped cucumber, diced scallions, all the egg yolks, and most of the egg white, reserving a little to sprinkle over the tops. Flake in the tuna.

6 Add 1 tablespoon of the mayonnaise, the lemon juice, and salt and pepper to taste. Stir together and add a little more mayonnaise if the mixture is too thick. Tear in the basil leaves and stir together. Adjust the seasoning, if necessary.

7 Spoon the filling into the hollowed-out tomatoes. Sprinkle

the tops with the reserved egg white. Cover with plastic wrap and chill until required, but not for more than 3 hours or the filling will become soggy. Garnish with basil leaves before serving.

smoked trout with pears

serves four

1¼ cups watercress or arugula

1 head of radicchio, torn into pieces

4 smoked trout fillets, skinned

2 ripe pears, such as Bartlett

2 tbsp lemon juice

2 tbsp extra-virgin olive oil

salt and pepper

3 tbsp sour cream

2 tsp creamed horseradish

thinly sliced brown bread, crusts removed and buttered, to serve

VARIATION

Replace the horseradish with mustard mayonnaise. Mix 3 teaspoons mustard, 2 teaspoons chopped fresh dill, and ⅔ cup mayonnaise. Season.

1 Place the watercress and radicchio in a bowl. Cut the trout fillets into thin strips and add to the bowl. Halve and core the pears, then slice thinly. Place in a separate bowl, add 4 teaspoons of the lemon juice, and toss to coat. Add the pears to the salad.

2 To make the dressing, mix the remaining lemon juice and the olive oil together in a bowl, then season to taste with salt and pepper. Pour the dressing over the salad and toss well. Transfer to a large salad bowl.

3 Mix the sour cream and horseradish together in a separate bowl until thoroughly blended, then spoon over the salad. Serve with buttered brown bread.

sweet & sour fish salad

serves four

8 oz/225 g trout fillets

8 oz/225 g white fish fillets (such as haddock or cod)

1¼ cups water

1 stem lemon-grass

2 lime leaves

1 large red chili

1 bunch scallions, trimmed and shredded

4 oz/115 g fresh pineapple flesh, diced

1 small red bell pepper, deseeded and diced

1 bunch watercress, washed and trimmed

fresh snipped chives, to garnish

DRESSING

1 tbsp sunflower oil

1 tbsp rice wine vinegar

pinch of chili powder

1 tsp clear honey

salt and pepper

1 Rinse the fish, place in a skillet and pour over the water. Bend the lemongrass in half to bruise it and add to the skillet with the lime leaves. Prick the chili with a fork and add to the pan. Bring to a boil and simmer for 7-8 minutes. Let cool.

2 Drain the fish fillet thoroughly, then flake the flesh away from the skin and place it in a bowl. Gently stir in the scallions, pineapple and bell pepper.

3 Arrange the washed watercress on 4 serving plates and spoon the cooked fish mixture on top.

4 To make the sweet-and-sour dressing, mix all the ingredients together and season well. Spoon it over the fish and serve the salad garnished with chives.

COOK'S TIP

This recipe also works very well if you replace the fish with 12 ounces white crabmeat. Add a dash of Tabasco sauce if you like it hot!

mackerel & potato salad

serves four

4½ oz/125 g new potatoes,
    scrubbed and diced

8 oz/225 g mackerel fillets, skinned

5 cups water

1 bay leaf

1 slice of lemon

1 eating apple, cored and diced

1 shallot, thinly sliced

3 tbsp white wine vinegar

1 tsp corn oil

1½ tsp superfine sugar

¼ tsp Dijon mustard

salt and pepper

TO SERVE

2 tbsp lowfat plain yogurt

¼ cucumber, thinly sliced

1 tbsp snipped fresh chives

1 bunch of arugula

COOK'S TIP

If new potatoes are not in
season, use a waxy,
firm-fleshed potato, such as
round red, round white, or
All Blue potatoes instead.

1 Steam the potatoes over a pan of simmering water for 10 minutes, or until tender. Meanwhile, using a sharp knife, remove the skin from the mackerel fillets and cut into bite-size pieces. Bring the water to a boil in a large, shallow pan, then reduce the heat so that it is just simmering and add the mackerel pieces, bay leaf, and lemon. Poach for 3 minutes, or until the flesh is opaque. Remove the mackerel from the pan with a spatula and transfer to a serving dish.

2 Drain the potatoes well and transfer them to a large bowl. Mix with the apple and shallot, then spoon the mixture over the mackerel.

3 Mix the vinegar, oil sugar, and mustard together in a measuring cup, season to taste with salt and pepper and whisk well. Pour the dressing over the potato mixture. Cover and chill in the refrigerator for up to 6 hours.

4 To serve, spread the yogurt over the salad, then arrange the cucumber decoratively on top and sprinkle with the fresh chives. Surround the salad with the arugula.

VARIATION

Fresh salmon is very versatile
and would work equally well
in this dish. Replace the mackerel
fillets with the same quantity
of salmon fillets.

cantaloupe & crab salad

serves four

12 oz/350 g fresh crabmeat

5 tbsp lowfat mayonnaise

¼ cup lowfat plain yogurt

4 tsp extra-virgin olive oil

4 tsp lime juice

1 scallion, finely chopped

4 tsp finely chopped fresh parsley

pinch of cayenne pepper

1 cantaloupe melon

2 radicchio heads, separated
   into leaves

fresh parsley sprigs, to garnish

1 Place the crabmeat in a large bowl and pick over it very carefully to remove any remaining shell or cartilage, but try not to break the meat up.

2 Put the lowfat mayonnaise, yogurt, olive oil, lime juice, scallion, chopped fresh parsley, and cayenne pepper into a separate bowl and mix until thoroughly blended. Fold in the crabmeat.

3 Cut the melon in half and remove and discard the seeds. Thinly slice, then cut off the rind with a sharp knife.

4 Arrange the melon slices and radicchio leaves on 4 large serving plates, then arrange the crabmeat mixture on top. Garnish with a few sprigs of fresh parsley and serve.

COOK'S TIP

If fresh crabmeat is not available, you can use frozen crabmeat. Let the crab thaw thoroughly before making the salad.

lobster & avocado salad

serves four

2 x 14 oz/400 g cooked lobsters

1 large avocado

1 tbsp lemon juice

8 oz/225 g green beans

4 scallions, thinly sliced

2 tbsp chopped fresh chervil

1 tbsp chopped fresh chives

DRESSING

1 garlic clove, crushed

1 tsp Dijon mustard

pinch of sugar

1 tbsp balsamic vinegar

5 tbsp olive oil

salt and pepper

COOK'S TIP

When buying a whole cooked lobster, look for bright shiny eyes, firm flesh, a pleasant aroma and curled tail. This indicates it was alive when cooked.

1 To prepare the lobsters, cut them in half lengthwise. Remove the intestinal vein which runs down the tail, the stomach sac, and any gray beards from the body cavity at the head end of the lobster. Crack the claws and remove the meat—in one piece if possible. Remove the meat from the tail of the lobster. Coarsely chop all the meat and set aside.

2 Split the avocado lengthwise and remove the pit. Cut each half in half again and peel off the skin. Cut the avocado flesh into chunks and toss with the lemon juice to prevent it from discoloring. Add to the lobster meat.

3 Bring a large pan of lightly salted water to a boil and add the green beans. Cook for 3 minutes, then drain, and immediately refresh under cold water. Drain again and set aside to cool completely. Cut the beans in half, then add them to the avocado and lobster.

4 Meanwhile, make the dressing by whisking together the garlic, mustard, sugar, vinegar, and seasoning. Gradually add the oil, whisking, until thickened.

5 Add the scallions, chervil, and chives to the lobster and avocado mixture and toss gently together. Drizzle over the dressing and serve immediately.

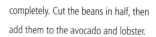

113

smoked haddock salad

serves four

12 oz/350 g smoked haddock fillet

4 tbsp olive oil

1 tbsp lemon juice

2 tbsp sour cream

1 tbsp hot water

2 tbsp chopped fresh chives,
    plus extra to garnish

1 plum tomato, skinned, deseeded,
    and diced

8 quail eggs

4 thick slices whole-wheat or
    multigrain bread

4 oz/115 g mixed salad greens

salt and pepper

1 Fill a large skillet with water and bring to a boil. Add the fish, cover, and remove from the heat. Set aside for 10 minutes until the fish is tender. Lift out the fish, drain, and set aside until cool enough to handle. Flake the flesh, removing any small bones. Discard the poaching water.

COOK'S TIP

When buying smoked haddock, and smoked fish in general, look for undyed fish, which is always superior in quality.

2 Whisk together the olive oil, lemon juice, sour cream, hot water, and chives and season to taste with salt and pepper. Stir in the tomato. Set aside.

3 Bring a small pan of water to a boil. Carefully lower the quail eggs into the water. Bring back to a boil and cook the eggs for 3–4 minutes (3 minutes for a slightly soft center, 4 minutes for a firm center). Drain immediately and refresh under cold running water until cold. Carefully shell the eggs, cut in half lengthwise, and set aside.

4 Toast the bread and cut each slice diagonally to form 4 triangles. Arrange 2 halves on each of 4 serving plates. Top with the salad greens, then the flaked fish, and finally the quail eggs. Spoon over the dressing and garnish with a few extra chives.

skate & spinach salad

serves four

1 lb 9 oz/700 g skate wings, trimmed

2 fresh rosemary sprigs

1 fresh bay leaf

1 tbsp black peppercorns

1 lemon, quartered

1 lb/450 g baby spinach leaves

1 tbsp olive oil

1 small red onion, thinly sliced

2 garlic cloves, crushed

½ tsp chili flakes

½ cup pine nuts, lightly toasted

⅓ cup raisins

1 tbsp light molasses sugar

2 tbsp chopped fresh parsley

1 Put the skate into a large saucepan with the herbs, peppercorns, and lemon. Cover with water and bring to a boil. Cover and simmer for 4–5 minutes until the flesh begins to come away from the cartilage. Remove from the heat and set aside for 15 minutes. Lift the fish from the water and remove the flesh in shreds.

2 Meanwhile, put the spinach into a pan with just the water that clings to the leaves. Cook over high heat for 30 seconds until wilted. Drain, refresh under cold water and drain again. Squeeze out any excess water and set aside.

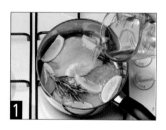

3 Heat the oil in a large skillet. Cook the onion for 3–4 minutes until softened, but not browned. Add the garlic, chili flakes, pine nuts, raisins, and sugar. Cook for 1–2 minutes, then add the spinach and toss for 1 minute until heated through. Gently fold in the skate and cook for a further minute. Season well.

4 Divide the salad among 4 serving plates and sprinkle with the parsley.

ceviche

COOK'S TIP

As the scallops are marinated and
not cooked it is essential to use
the freshest scallops possible.

1 If the scallops are in shells, use an oyster knife or small knife to prize the shells open, then rinse under running cold water. Cut the scallops and coral free from the shells. Slice the scallop flesh into 2–3 horizontal slices each. Place in a nonmetallic bowl with the corals.

2 Remove the heads and peel the shrimp. Using a small sharp knife, devein them. Add to the scallops.

3 Cut the sea bass fillet into thin slices across the grain and add to the bowl of seafood.

4 Firmly roll the lemon and lime backward and forward on a counter to help release the juice. Cut the lemon in half and squeeze the juice over the fish. Repeat with the lime.

5 Gently stir to coat the seafood well in the citrus juices, then cover with plastic wrap, and chill in the refrigerator for 2 hours or until the seafood becomes opaque, but do not leave for longer otherwise the seafood will be too soft.

6 Using a slotted spoon, transfer the seafood to another bowl. Add the onion, chili, and olive oil and stir gently. Set aside at room temperature for about 5 minutes.

7 Spoon the seafood onto individual serving plates and serve immediately with salad greens, lemon or lime wedges, and black pepper.

seafood & spinach salad

serves four

1 lb 2 oz/500 g live mussels, soaked
and cleaned

3½ oz/100 g shrimp, peeled and
deveined

12 oz/350 g scallops

1 lb 2 oz/500 g baby spinach leaves

3 scallions, trimmed and sliced

DRESSING

4 tbsp extra-virgin olive oil

2 tbsp white wine vinegar

1 tbsp lemon juice

1 tsp finely grated lemon zest

1 garlic clove, chopped

1 tbsp grated fresh gingerroot

1 small red chili, seeded and sliced

1 tbsp chopped fresh cilantro

salt and pepper

GARNISH

sprigs of fresh cilantro

wedges of lemon

COOK'S TIP

To store spinach, leave packaged
spinach in its cellophane bag,
or pack it loosely in a plastic bag
and store in the refrigerator
crisper. Fresh spinach will keep
for three to four days.

1 Put the mussels into a large pan
with a little water, bring to a boil,
and cook over high heat for 4 minutes.
Drain and reserve the liquid. Discard
any mussels that remain closed. Return
the reserved liquid to the pan and
bring to a boil. Add the shrimp and
scallops and cook for 3 minutes. Drain.
Remove the mussels from their shells.
Rinse the mussels, shrimp, and scallops
in cold water, drain, and put them in a
large bowl. Cool, cover with plastic
wrap, and chill for 45 minutes.
Meanwhile, rinse the baby spinach
leaves and transfer them to a pan

with 4 tablespoons of water. Cook
over high heat for 1 minute, transfer
to a strainer, refresh under cold
running water, and drain.

2 To make the dressing, put all the
ingredients into a small bowl and
mix. Arrange the spinach on serving
dishes, then scatter over half of the
scallions. Top with the mussels, shrimp
and scallops, then scatter over the
remaining scallions. Drizzle over the
dressing, garnish with fresh cilantro
sprigs and wedges of lemon, and serve.

neapolitan seafood salad

serves four

1 lb prepared squid, cut into strips

1 lb/10 oz cooked mussels

1 lb cooked cockles in brine

⅝ cup white wine

1½ cups olive oil

2 cups dried campanelle or other
   small pasta shapes

juice of 1 lemon

1 bunch chives, snipped

1 bunch fresh parsley, finely
   chopped

4 large tomatoes, cut into fourths
   or sliced

mixed salad greens

salt and pepper

sprig of fresh basil, to garnish

1 Put all of the seafood into a large bowl. Pour over the wine and half the olive oil, then set aside for 6 hours.

2 Put the seafood mixture into a saucepan and simmer over a low heat for 10 minutes. Set aside to cool.

3 Bring a large saucepan of lightly salted water to a boil. Add the pasta and 1 tbsp of the remaining olive oil and cook until tender, but still firm to the bite. Drain thoroughly and refresh in cold water.

VARIATION

You can substitute cooked scallops for the mussels and clams in brine for the cockles, if you prefer. The seafood needs to be marinated for 6 hours, so prepare well in advance.

4 Strain off about half of the cooking liquid from the seafood and discard the rest. Mix in the

lemon juice, chives, parsley, and the remaining olive oil. Season to taste with salt and pepper. Drain the pasta and add to the seafood.

5 Cut the tomatoes into fourths. Shred the salad greens and arrange them at the base of a salad bowl. Spoon in the seafood salad and garnish with the tomatoes and a sprig of basil.

caesar salad

⅔ cup olive oil

2 garlic cloves

5 slices white bread, crusts removed,
cut into ½-inch/1-cm cubes

1 large egg

2 Romaine lettuces or
3 Boston lettuces

2 tbsp lemon juice

salt and pepper

8 canned anchovy fillets, drained
and coarsely chopped

¾ cup fresh Parmesan cheese
shavings

1 Bring a small, heavy-bottom pan of water to a boil.

2 Meanwhile, heat 4 tablespoons of the olive oil in a heavy-bottom skillet. Add the garlic and diced bread and cook, stirring and tossing frequently, for 4–5 minutes, or until the bread is crispy and golden all over. Remove from the skillet with a slotted spoon and drain on paper towels.

3 Add the egg to the boiling water and cook for 1 minute, then remove from the pan and set aside.

4 Arrange the lettuce leaves in a salad bowl. Mix the remaining olive oil and lemon juice together, then season to taste with salt and pepper. Crack the egg into the dressing and whisk to blend. Pour the dressing over the lettuce leaves, toss well, then add the croutons and anchovies and toss the salad again. Sprinkle with Parmesan cheese shavings and serve.

VARIATION

Replace the Romaine and Boston lettuces with mixed salad greens, such as lollo rosso, oak leaf, and arugula.

panzanella

serves four–six

9 oz stale Herb Foccacia or ciabatta
   bread or French bread

4 large, vine-ripened tomatoes

extra-virgin olive oil

4 red, yellow, and/or orange
   bell peppers

3½ oz cucumber

1 large red onion, finely chopped

8 canned anchovy fillets, drained
   and chopped

2 tbsp capers in brine, rinsed and
   patted dry

about 4 tbsp red wine vinegar

about 2 tbsp best-quality
   balsamic vinegar

salt and pepper

fresh basil leaves, to garnish

1 Cut the bread into 1-inch cubes and place in a large bowl. Working over a plate to catch any juices, quarter the tomatoes; reserve the juices. Using a teaspoon, scoop out the cores and seeds, then finely chop the flesh. Add to the bread cubes.

2 Drizzle 5 tablespoons of olive oil over the mixture and toss with your hands until well coated. Pour in the reserved tomato juice and toss again. Set aside for about 30 minutes.

3 Meanwhile, cut the bell peppers in half and remove the cores and seeds. Place on a broiler rack under a preheated hot broiler and broil for 10 minutes, or until the skins are charred and the flesh softened. Place in a plastic bag, seal, and set aside for 20 minutes to allow the steam to loosen the skins. Remove the skins, then finely chop.

4 Cut the cucumber in half lengthwise, then cut each half into 3 strips lengthwise. Using a teaspoon, scoop out and discard the seeds. Dice the cucumber.

5 Add the onion, peppers, cucumber, anchovy fillets, and capers to the bread and toss together. Sprinkle with the red wine and balsamic vinegars and season to taste with salt and pepper. Drizzle with extra olive oil or vinegar if necessary, but be cautious that it does not become too greasy or soggy. Sprinkle the fresh basil leaves over the salad and serve at once.

mussel salad

serves four

2 red bell peppers, halved
and seeded

12 oz/350 g cooked, shelled
mussels, thawed if frozen

1 head radicchio

¾ cup arugula

8 cooked green-lipped mussels in
their shells

strips of lemon peel, to garnish

crusty bread, to serve

DRESSING

1 tbsp olive oil

1 tbsp lemon juice

1 tsp finely grated lemon peel

2 tsp honey

1 tsp French mustard

1 tbsp snipped fresh chives

salt and pepper

COOK'S TIP

Olive oil is very versatile as it
can be used for sautéing,
cooking, and salad dressings.
Use the best-quality extra-virgin
olive oil that you can find in
dressings and use the ordinary
virgin olive oil in cooking.

1 Put the bell peppers, skin-side up, on a broiler rack and cook under a preheated broiler for 8–10 minutes, or until the skin is charred and blistered and the flesh is soft. Remove from the broiler with tongs, put into a bowl, and cover with plastic wrap. Set aside for 10 minutes, or until cool enough to handle, then peel off the skins.

2 Slice the bell pepper flesh into thin strips and put into a bowl. Gently stir in the shelled mussels.

3 To make the dressing, whisk the oil, lemon juice and peel, honey, mustard, and chives together until well blended. Season to taste with salt and pepper. Add the bell pepper and mussel mixture and toss until coated.

4 Remove the central core of the radicchio and shred the leaves. Put into a serving bowl with the arugula and toss together.

5 Pile the mussel mixture into the center of the leaves and arrange the green-lipped mussels in their shells around the edge. Garnish with lemon peel and serve with crusty bread.

traditional catalan salt cod salad

serves four–six

14 oz/400 g dried salt cod in
  1 piece
6 scallions, thinly sliced on
  the diagonal
6 tbsp extra-virgin olive oil
1 tbsp sherry vinegar
1 tbsp lemon juice
2 large red bell peppers, broiled,
  peeled, seeded, and very
  finely diced
12 large black olives, pitted
  and sliced
2 large, juicy tomatoes, thinly sliced
pepper
2 tbsp very finely chopped fresh
  parsley, to garnish

1 Place the dried salt cod in a large
  bowl, then cover with cold water
and let soak for 48 hours, changing the
water 3 times a day.

COOK'S TIP

To prepare an updated version
of this salad, place the desalted
salt cod in the freezer for
30 minutes, then thinly slice.
(If you try to slice the salt cod
without freezing first, the slices
will fall apart.)

2 Pat the salt cod very dry with
  paper towels and remove the skin
and bones, then use your fingers to
tear into fine shreds. Place in a large,
nonmetallic bowl with the scallions,
olive oil, vinegar, and lemon juice and
toss together. Season with pepper,
then cover and let marinate in the
refrigerator for 3 hours.

3 Stir in the bell peppers and olives.
  Taste and adjust the seasoning, if
necessary, remembering that the cod
and olives might be salty. Arrange the
tomato slices on a large serving platter
or individual serving plates and spoon
the salad on top. Sprinkle with
chopped parsley and serve.

VARIATION

For a summer tapas, cut
vine-ripened cherry tomatoes in
half and use a teaspoon to scoop
out the seeds. Sprinkle with sea
salt and turn upside down
on paper towels to drain for
30 minutes. Spoon the salad into
the tomato halves and sprinkle
with parsley.

tuna, egg & potato salad

serves four

12 oz/350 g new potatoes,
   unpeeled

1 hard-cooked egg, cooled
   and shelled

3 tbsp olive oil

1½ tbsp white wine vinegar

4 oz/115 g canned tuna in oil,
   drained and flaked

2 shallots, finely chopped

1 tomato, peeled and diced

2 tbsp chopped fresh parsley

salt and pepper

VARIATION

This salad is even more delicious
if it is made with fresh tuna that
has been griddled for 2 minutes
on each side, then diced.

1 Cook the potatoes in a pan of lightly salted boiling water for 10 minutes, then remove from the heat, cover, and let stand for 15–20 minutes, or until tender.

2 Meanwhile, slice the egg, then cut each slice in half. Whisk the olive oil and vinegar together in a bowl and season to taste with salt and pepper. Spoon a little of the vinaigrette into a serving dish to coat the base.

3 Drain the potatoes, then peel and thinly slice. Place half the slices over the base of the dish and season to taste with salt, then top with half the tuna, half the egg slices, and half the shallots. Pour over half the remaining dressing. Make a second layer with the remaining potato slices, tuna, egg, and shallots, then pour over the remaining dressing.

4 Finally, top the salad with the tomato and parsley. Cover with plastic wrap and let stand in a cool place for 1–2 hours before serving.

Vegetarian Salads

Vegetarian salads are among the most evocative. The mere sight of a plate of Greek Feta Salad (see page 134) immediately transports the mind to a sun-kissed Aegean island, while the heady aroma of herbs and lemon wafting from a bowl of Tabbouleh (see page 170) conjures up the sights and sounds of the bustling streets of a Middle Eastern bazaar, and Asian Lettuce Cups (see page 165) will bring an exotic touch to the table. Perhaps not all the salads in this chapter are quite so reminiscent of other lands and happy vacations, although there are quite a few, but they do paint colorful pictures on the plate. More important still, they taste exquisite, whether based on pasta and noodles, rice and other grains, beans and lentils, cheese and nuts, or fruit and vegetables. And, of course, you don't have to be a vegetarian to enjoy them.

hot & sour noodle & mushroom salad

serves four

9 oz/250 g rice vermicelli noodles

2 tbsp sesame oil

6 scallions

6 oz/175 g white mushrooms

½ cucumber

DRESSING

4 tbsp sesame oil

2 tbsp soya sauce

juice of 2 limes

1 tsp sugar

1–2 tsp hot chili sauce

2 tbsp chopped fresh cilantro

1 Soak the noodles in a bowl of hot water for 10 minutes, or according to the package instructions. Drain and place in a large bowl. Add the sesame oil and toss until the noodles are coated with the oil.

2 Slice the scallions and mushrooms, then cut the cucumber into short thin sticks. Add to the noodles in the bowl.

3 To make the dressing, place the sesame oil, fish sauce, lime juice, sugar, and chili sauce in a small bowl and whisk together. Stir in the chopped cilantro.

4 Pour the dressing over the salad and toss until coated. Serve at once.

VARIATION

This dish is also excellent made with thick Thai noodles, which give a more robust texture.

avocado salad with lime dressing

serves four

2¼ oz/60 g mixed fresh red and
　　green lettuce leaves
2¼ oz/60 g fresh arugula
4 scallions, finely diced
5 tomatoes, sliced
¼ cup chopped walnuts, toasted
2 avocados
1 tbsp lemon juice
LIME DRESSING
1 tbsp lime juice
1 tsp Dijon mustard
1 tbsp crème fraîche or sour cream
1 tbsp chopped fresh parsley
　　or cilantro
3 tbsp extra-virgin olive oil
pinch of sugar
salt and pepper

1 Wash and drain the lettuce and arugula, if necessary. Shred all the leaves and arrange in the bottom of a large salad bowl. Add the scallions, tomatoes, and walnuts.

2 Halve, peel, and pit the avocados and cut into thin slices or small chunks. Brush with the lemon juice to prevent discoloration, then transfer to the salad bowl. Mix together gently.

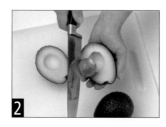

3 Put the dressing ingredients into a screw-top jar, screw on the lid tightly, and shake well until thoroughly combined. Drizzle the dressing over the salad and serve immediately.

COOK'S TIP
Don't leave the salad standing around too long after the dressing has been added or the lettuce will go soggy and the salad will be unusable.

greek feta salad

serves four

DRESSING

3 tbsp extra-virgin olive oil

1 tbsp lemon juice

½ tsp dried oregano

salt and pepper

4 tomatoes, sliced

½ cucumber, peeled and sliced

1 small red onion, sliced thinly

4 oz/115 g feta cheese, cubed

8 black olives

a few grape leaves, to serve

1 Peel and slice the cucumber. Cut the feta cheese into cubes. To make the dressing, put the oil, lemon juice, oregano, salt, and pepper in a screw-topped jar and shake together until blended.

2 Arrange the grape leaves on a serving dish and then the tomatoes, cucumber, and onion. Sprinkle the cheese and olives on top. Pour the dressing over the salad and serve.

VARIATION

If you want to move away from the traditional why not try a mixture of green and black olives to give a difference in color and flavor.

potato, arugula & mozzarella salad

serves four

1 lb 7 oz/650 g small new potatoes

4½ oz/125 g arugula

5½ oz/150 g firm mozzarella

1 large pear

1 tbsp lemon juice

salt and pepper

DRESSING

3 tbsp extra-virgin olive oil

1½ tbsp white wine vinegar

1 tsp sugar

pinch of mustard powder

1 Bring a pan of salted water to a boil. Add the potatoes, lower the heat, and cook for about 15 minutes, until tender. Remove from the heat, drain, and let cool.

2 When the potatoes are cool, cut them in half and place them in a large salad bowl. Wash and drain the arugula, cut the mozzarella into cubes, and wash, trim, and slice the pear. Add them to the bowl along with the lemon juice. Season with salt and pepper.

3 To make the dressing, mix together the oil, vinegar, sugar, and mustard powder. Pour the dressing over the salad and toss all the ingredients together until they are well coated. Serve at once.

VARIATION

To transform this dish in a trice, why not add some sunblushed tomatoes that have been stored in olive oil.

mexican tomato salad

serves four

1 lb 5 oz/600 g tomatoes, peeled,
 seeded, and coarsely chopped

1 onion, thinly sliced and pushed
 out into rings

14 oz/400 g canned kidney beans,
 drained and rinsed

1 fresh green chili, seeded and
 thinly sliced

3 tbsp chopped fresh cilantro

3 tbsp olive oil

1 garlic clove, finely chopped

4 tbsp lime juice

salt and pepper

1 Place the chopped tomatoes and onion slices into a large serving bowl and mix well. Stir in the kidney beans.

2 Mix the chili, cilantro, olive oil, garlic, and lime juice together in a measuring cup and season to taste with salt and pepper.

3 Pour the dressing over the salad and toss thoroughly. Serve immediately or cover with plastic wrap and let chill in the refrigerator until required.

VARIATION

You could substitute two canned chipotle chilies, drained and rinsed, for the fresh chili, and fava beans for the kidney beans, if you prefer.

warm pasta salad

serves four

8 oz/225 g dried farfalle or other
pasta shapes

6 pieces of sun-dried tomato in oil,
drained and chopped

4 scallions, chopped

1¼ cups arugula, shredded

½ cucumber, seeded and diced

salt and pepper

2 tbsp freshly grated Parmesan
cheese

DRESSING

4 tbsp olive oil

1 tbsp white wine vinegar

½ tsp superfine sugar

1 tsp Dijon mustard

salt and pepper

4 fresh basil leaves, finely shredded

COOK'S TIP

It makes it easier to toss the
pasta if you use 2 forks or
2 dessertspoons, and before
adding the dressing to the
salad, whisk it again until
emulsified. Add the dressing
just before serving.

1 To make the dressing, whisk the olive oil, vinegar, sugar, and mustard together in a bowl or pitcher. Season to taste with salt and pepper and stir in the basil.

2 Bring a large heavy-bottom pan of lightly salted water to a boil. Add the pasta, return to a boil, and cook for 8–10 minutes, or until tender but still firm to the bite. Drain and transfer to a salad bowl. Add the dressing and toss well.

3 Add the tomatoes, scallions, arugula, and cucumber, season to taste with salt and pepper, and toss. Sprinkle with the Parmesan cheese and serve warm.

spinach & orange salad

serves four–six

8 oz/225 g fresh baby spinach
  leaves

2 large oranges

½ red onion

DRESSING

3 tbsp extra-virgin olive oil

2 tbsp freshly squeezed orange juice

2 tsp lemon juice

1 tsp clear honey

½ tsp whole-grain mustard

salt and pepper

COOK'S TIP

Tear the spinach leaves into
bite-size pieces rather than
cutting them because cutting
bruises the leaves.

1 Wash the spinach leaves under cold running water and dry them thoroughly on paper towels. Remove and discard any tough stems and tear the larger leaves into smaller pieces.

2 Slice the top and bottom off each orange with a sharp knife, then remove the peel. Carefully slice between the membranes of the orange to remove the segments.

3 Using a sharp knife, finely chop the onion. Mix the salad greens and orange segments together and arrange in a serving dish. Scatter the chopped onion over the salad.

4 To make the dressing, whisk the olive oil, orange juice, lemon juice, honey, mustard, and salt and pepper to taste together in a small bowl. Pour the dressing over the salad just before serving. Toss the salad well to coat the greens with the dressing.

warm lentil salad with balsamic dressing

serves six–eight

scant 1 cup Puy lentils, cooked
(see Cook's Tip)

4 tbsp olive oil

1 small onion, sliced

4 celery stalks, sliced

2 garlic cloves, crushed

2 zucchinis, trimmed and diced

4½ oz/125 g green beans,
cut into short lengths

½ red bell pepper, seeded and diced

½ yellow bell pepper, seeded
and diced

1 tsp Dijon mustard

1 tbsp balsamic vinegar

salt and pepper

COOK'S TIP

To cook the lentils, rinse, and
place in a large pan. Cover with
plenty of cold water and bring
to a boil. Boil rapidly for
10 minutes, then simmer for
20 minutes until tender. Drain well.

1 Place the lentils in a large bowl.
The lentils can still be warm, if
wished.

2 Heat the olive oil in a pan. Add
the onion and celery and cook for
2–3 minutes, until softened but not
browned.

3 Stir the garlic, zucchinis, and
green beans into the pan and
cook for an additional 2 minutes.
Add the bell peppers and cook
for 1 minute.

VARIATION

Replace the Dijon mustard with
whole-grain and use a red onion
instead of an ordinary one.

4 Stir the mustard and the balsamic
vinegar into the pan and mix until
warm and well combined.

5 Pour the warm mixture over the
lentils and toss together to mix
well. Season to taste with salt and
pepper and serve immediately.

italian salad

serves four

8 oz/225 g dried conchiglie

1¾ oz/50 g pine nuts

12 oz/350 g cherry tomatoes,
    cut in half

1 red bell pepper, seeded and
    cut into bite-size chunks

1 red onion, chopped

7 oz/200 g buffalo mozzarella, cubed

12 black olives, pitted

1 oz/25 g fresh basil leaves

DRESSING

5 tbsp extra-virgin olive oil

2 tbsp balsamic vinegar

1 tbsp chopped fresh basil

salt and pepper

shavings of fresh Parmesan,
    to garnish

COOK'S TIP

Basil originates from India
where it is considered sacred
to the Gods. It is best to use fresh
basil, and even better to grown
your own.

1 Bring a large pan of lightly salted water to a boil. Add the pasta and cook over medium heat for about 10 minutes, or according to the package instructions. When cooked, the pasta should be tender but still firm to the bite. Drain, rinse under cold running water, and drain again. Let cool.

2 While the pasta is cooking, put the pine nuts in a dry skillet and cook over low heat for 1–2 minutes, until golden brown. Remove from the heat, transfer to a dish, and let cool.

3 To make the dressing, put the oil, vinegar, and basil into a small bowl. Season with salt and pepper and stir together well. Cover with plastic wrap and set to one side.

4 To assemble the salad, divide the pasta between serving bowls. Add the pine nuts, tomatoes, red bell pepper, onion, cheese, and olives. Scatter over the basil leaves, then drizzle over the dressing. Garnish with fresh Parmesan shavings and serve.

pasta salad with basil vinaigrette

serves four

8 oz/225 g dried fusilli

salt and pepper

4 tomatoes

scant ⅓ cup black olives

1 oz/25 g sun-dried tomatoes in oil

2 tbsp pine nuts

2 tbsp freshly grated Parmesan
  cheese

fresh basil leaves, to garnish

VINAIGRETTE

½ oz/15 g basil leaves

1 garlic clove, crushed

2 tbsp freshly grated Parmesan
  cheese

4 tbsp extra-virgin olive oil

2 tbsp lemon juice

1 Cook the pasta in a large pan of lightly salted boiling water for 10–12 minutes, or until just tender but still firm to the bite. Drain the pasta, rinse under cold running water, then drain again thoroughly. Place the pasta in a large bowl.

2 Preheat the broiler to medium. To make the vinaigrette, place the basil leaves, garlic, cheese, olive oil, and lemon juice in a food processor. Season to taste with salt and pepper and process until the leaves are well chopped and the ingredients are combined. Alternatively, finely chop the basil leaves by hand and combine with the other vinaigrette ingredients. Pour the vinaigrette over the pasta and toss to coat.

3 Cut the tomatoes into wedges. Pit and halve the olives. Slice the sun-dried tomatoes. Toast the pine nuts on a cookie sheet under the hot broiler until golden.

4 Add the tomatoes (fresh and sun-dried) and the olives to the pasta and mix until combined.

5 Transfer the pasta to a serving dish, sprinkle over the Parmesan and toasted pine nuts and serve garnished with a few basil leaves.

mango & wild rice salad

serves four

generous ⅓ cup wild rice

¾ cup basmati rice

salt and pepper

3 tbsp hazelnut oil

1 tbsp sherry vinegar

1 ripe mango

3 celery stalks

2¾ oz/75 g oz no-soak dried
    apricots, chopped

¾ cup slivered almonds, toasted

2 tbsp chopped fresh cilantro

fresh cilantro sprigs, to garnish

1 Cook the rice in separate large pans in lightly salted boiling water. Cook the wild rice for 45–50 minutes and the basmati rice for 10–12 minutes. Drain, rinse well, and drain again. Place the cooked rice in a large bowl.

2 Mix together the hazelnut oil, vinegar, and salt and pepper to taste. Pour the mixture over the rice and toss well.

3 Cut the mango in half lengthwise, as close to the pit as possible. Remove and discard the pit.

4 Peel the skin from the mango and cut the flesh into slices.

5 Slice the celery thinly and add to the cooled rice with the mango, apricots, almonds, and chopped cilantro. Toss together and transfer to a serving dish. Garnish with cilantro sprigs.

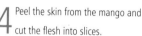

COOK'S TIP

To toast almonds, place them on a large cookie sheet in a preheated oven at 350°F/ 180°C for 5–10 minutes. Alternatively, toast them under a preheated hot broiler, turning frequently.

VARIATION

Replace the fresh cilantro with the same amount of fresh mint and use mint sprigs to garnish, if you prefer.

147

tricolor pasta salad

serves four

salt and pepper

6 oz/175 g dried fusilli

1 avocado

6 tomatoes, thinly sliced

8 oz/225 g mozzarella cheese,
    thinly sliced

2 tbsp toasted pine nuts

fresh basil leaves, to garnish

DRESSING

6 tbsp extra-virgin olive oil

2 tbsp white wine vinegar

1 tsp Dijon mustard

2 tbsp shredded fresh basil leaves

pinch of sugar

1 Bring a large pan of lightly salted water to a boil. Add the pasta, return to the boil, and cook for 8–10 minutes, or until tender but still firm to the bite. Drain, refresh under cold running water, and drain again.

2 To make the dressing, whisk the oil, vinegar, mustard, basil, and sugar together in a small bowl until combined. Season to taste with salt and pepper.

3 Cut the avocado in half and remove the stone. Peel, then thinly slice the flesh lengthwise.

4 Arrange the slices of avocado, tomato, and mozzarella cheese, overlapping slightly, around the outside of a large serving platter. Add half the dressing to the pasta, toss well, then spoon into the center of the platter. Pour the remaining dressing over the salad, sprinkle with the pine nuts, garnish with basil leaves, and serve.

buckwheat noodle salad with smoked tofu

serves two

7 oz/200 g buckwheat noodles

9 oz/250 g firm smoked tofu (drained weight)

7 oz/200 g white cabbage, finely shredded

9 oz/250 g carrots, finely shredded

3 scallions, diagonally sliced

1 fresh red chili, seeded and finely sliced into circles

2 tbsp sesame seeds, lightly toasted

FOR THE DRESSING

1 tsp grated fresh gingerroot

1 garlic clove, crushed

6 oz/175 g silken tofu (drained weight)

4 tsp tamari (wheat-free soy sauce)

2 tbsp sesame oil

4 tbsp hot water

salt

COOK'S TIP

To toast the sesame seeds, gently dry-fry in a pan until lightly golden.

1 Cook the noodles in a large pan of lightly salted boiling water according to the package instructions. Drain and refresh under cold running water.

2 To make the dressing, blend the ginger, garlic, silken tofu, soy sauce, oil, and water together in a small bowl until smooth and creamy. Season to taste with salt.

3 Place the smoked tofu in a steamer. Steam for 5 minutes, then cut into thin slices.

4 Meanwhile, put the cabbage, carrots, scallions, and chili into a bowl and toss to mix. To serve, arrange the noodles on serving plates and top with the carrot salad and slices of tofu. Spoon over the dressing and sprinkle with sesame seeds.

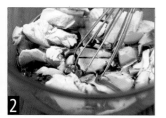

chicory, walnut & goat cheese salad

serves four

14 oz/400 g chicory

scant 1 cup walnut pieces

seeds from 1 pomegranate

2 tbsp walnut oil

2 tsp red wine vinegar

1 tsp Dijon mustard

pepper

4 slices whole-wheat bread

2 garlic cloves, halved

4 x 3½-oz/100 g goat cheeses,
   with rind

3 tsp olive oil

COOK'S TIP

Make sure you keep an eye on
the goat cheese while broiling,
as "nicely browned" can quickly
become "burned"!

---

1 Divide the heads of chicory into leaves and rinse, pat dry with paper towels, and arrange on 4 serving plates. Sprinkle over the walnut pieces and pomegranate seeds.

2 To make the dressing, whisk the walnut oil with the vinegar and mustard in a small bowl. Season with pepper and set aside.

3 Preheat the broiler to high. Rub the bread with the garlic. Arrange the goat cheeses on a sheet of foil and place on the broiler pan with the bread alongside. Cook under the preheated

broiler until the bread is toasted on both sides and the cheese is bubbling.

4 To serve, drizzle each toasted bread slice with the olive oil, and top with a goat cheese. Put one goat cheese toast on each salad and drizzle the whole dish with the dressing.

green bean & walnut salad

serves two

1 lb/450 g green beans

1 small onion, finely chopped

1 garlic clove, chopped

4 tbsp freshly grated Parmesan
  cheese

DRESSING

6 tbsp olive oil

2 tbsp white wine vinegar

salt and pepper

2 tsp chopped fresh tarragon

2 tbsp walnuts or almonds, to garnish

VARIATION

Replace the walnuts with
pine nuts for a variation in
texture and taste, and toast as
the recipe advises.

---

1 Trim the beans, but leave them whole. Cook for 3–4 minutes in salted boiling water. Drain well, refresh under cold running water, and drain again. Put into a mixing bowl and add the onion, garlic, and cheese.

2 Place the dressing ingredients in a jar with a screw-top lid. Shake well. Pour the dressing over the salad and toss gently to coat. Cover with plastic wrap and chill for at least 30 minutes.

3 Remove the beans from the refrigerator 10 minutes before serving. Give them a quick stir and transfer to an attractive, shallow serving dish.

4 Chop the nuts then toast in a dry skillet over medium heat for 2 minutes, or until they begin to brown. Sprinkle the toasted nuts over the beans to garnish before serving.

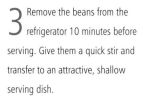

moroccan spiced salad

serves four

2 tbsp olive oil

scant ½ cup long-grain rice

1¾ cups water

4 tbsp lemon-flavored or
   extra-virgin olive oil

3 tbsp vinegar

1 tbsp lemon juice

1 tbsp honey

1 tsp garam masala

1 tsp ground coriander

½ tsp mustard

8 oz/225 g canned red kidney
   beans

8 oz/225 g canned garbanzos

2 shallots, chopped

4 scallions, trimmed and sliced

2¼ oz/60 g pine nuts

3½ oz/100 g golden raisins

1 tbsp chopped fresh mint

chopped fresh mint, to garnish

wedges of fresh lemon, to serve

1 Heat the olive oil in a large pan. Add the rice and cook for 3 minutes, stirring, over low heat. Pour in the water and bring to a boil, then lower the heat, cover, and simmer for 35 minutes. Remove from the heat and transfer to a strainer. Rinse under cold running water, drain well, and set aside to cool.

2 In a large bowl, mix together the lemon-flavored or extra-virgin olive oil, vinegar, lemon juice, and honey. Add the garam masala, coriander, and mustard and stir well.

3 Add the rice and mix well. Rinse and drain the kidney beans and garbanzos, then add them to the bowl with the shallots, scallions, pine nuts, golden raisins, and mint. Divide between serving bowls, garnish with chopped fresh mint, and serve with lemon wedges.

VARIATION
Try experimenting with different varieties of beans or, alternatively, a mixture of several types.

green bean salad with feta

serves four

12 oz/350 g green beans, trimmed

1 red onion, chopped

3–4 tbsp chopped fresh cilantro

2 radishes, thinly sliced

¾ cup crumbled feta cheese

1 tsp chopped fresh oregano or
   ½ tsp dried oregano

2 tbsp red wine or fruit vinegar

5 tbsp extra-virgin olive oil

3 ripe tomatoes, cut into wedges

pepper

1 Bring about 2 inches/5 cm water to a boil in the base of a steamer or in a medium saucepan. Add the green beans to the top of the steamer or place them in a metal colander set over the pan of water. Cover and steam for about 5 minutes until just tender.

2 Transfer the beans to a bowl and add the onion, cilantro, radishes, and crumbled feta cheese.

3 Sprinkle the oregano over the salad, then grind pepper over to taste. Whisk the vinegar and olive oil together and then pour over the salad. Toss gently to mix well.

4 Transfer to a serving platter, surround with the tomato wedges, and serve at once or chill until ready to serve.

VARIATION

This recipe is also delicious made with nopales, or edible cactus, which is available in specialist stores in cans or jars. Drain, then slice, and use instead of the green beans, missing out Step 1. Replace the feta with 1–2 chopped hard-cooked eggs.

three-bean salad

serves six

3 tbsp olive oil

1 tbsp lemon juice

1 tbsp tomato paste

1 tbsp light malt vinegar

1 tbsp chopped fresh chives, plus
extra to garnish

6 oz/175g thin green beans

14 oz/400 g can soybeans, rinsed
and drained

14 oz/400 g can red kidney beans,
rinsed and drained

2 tomatoes, chopped

4 scallions, trimmed and chopped

4½ oz/125 g feta cheese, cut into
cubes

salt and pepper

mixed salad greens, to serve

1 Put the olive oil, lemon juice, tomato paste, light malt vinegar, and chopped fresh chives into a large bowl and mix thoroughly. Set aside until required.

2 Cook the thin green beans in a small pan of lightly salted boiling water for 4–5 minutes. Drain, refresh under cold water to prevent any further cooking, and drain well again. Pat dry with absorbent paper towels.

3 Add all the beans to the dressing, stirring well to mix.

4 Add the tomatoes, scallions, and feta cheese to the bean mixture, tossing gently to coat in the dressing. Season to taste with salt and pepper.

5 Arrange the salad greens on serving plates. Pile the bean salad on top, garnish with extra chives, and serve.

broiled vegetable salad

serves four

1 zucchini, sliced

1 yellow bell pepper, deseeded
  and sliced

1 eggplant, sliced

1 fennel bulb, cut into 8 wedges

1 red onion, cut into 8 wedges

16 cherry tomatoes

3 tbsp olive oil

1 garlic clove, crushed

fresh rosemary sprigs, to garnish

DRESSING

4 tbsp olive oil

2 tbsp balsamic vinegar

2 tsp chopped fresh rosemary

1 tsp Dijon mustard

1 tsp honey

2 tsp lemon juice

1 Spread out all of the vegetables, except for the cherry tomatoes, on a cookie sheet.

2 Mix the oil and garlic and brush over the vegetables. Cook under a medium-hot broiler for 10 minutes until tender and beginning to char. Set aside to cool. Spoon the vegetables into a serving bowl with the cherry tomatoes.

3 Mix the dressing ingredients and pour over the vegetables. Cover and chill for 1 hour. Garnish and serve.

endive salad

serves four

1 pink grapefruit

1 avocado

2 oz/55 g mâche

2 heads endive, sliced diagonally

1 tbsp chopped fresh mint

FRENCH DRESSING

3 tbsp olive oil

1 tbsp wine vinegar

1 small garlic clove, crushed

½ tsp Dijon or Meaux mustard

1 tsp honey

salt and pepper

1 Peel the grapefruit with a serrated knife. Cut the grapefruit into segments by cutting between the membranes. Set aside.

2 To make the French dressing, put the oil, vinegar, garlic, mustard, and honey into a screw-top jar and shake vigorously. Season to taste with salt and pepper. Pour the dressing into a bowl.

3 Halve and pit the avocado and cut it into thin slices. Peel off the skin, cut the sliced flesh into the bowl of French dressing and toss gently to coat.

4 Remove any stems from the mâche and put into a bowl with the grapefruit, endive, and chopped mint.

5 Add the avocado slices and 2 tablespoons of the French dressing. Toss well and transfer to individual serving plates. Serve immediately.

COOK'S TIP
Mâche is also known as lamb's lettuce because the shape of its dark green leaves resembles a lamb's tongue. It is also known as corn salad. It is easy to grow in the garden and will withstand the frost.

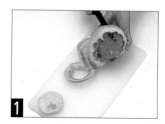

coronation salad

serves four

1 bell pepper

2 oz/⅓ cup golden raisins

1 celery stick, sliced

4½ oz/¾ cup sweetcorn

1 Granny Smith apple, diced

4½ oz/1 cup white seedless grapes,
washed and halved

9 oz/1½ cups cooked basmati rice

2 oz/½ cup cooked, peeled shrimp
(optional)

1 Romaine lettuce, washed
and drained

1 tsp paprika to garnish

DRESSING

4 tbsp lowfat mayonnaise

2 tsp mild curry powder

1 tsp lemon juice

1 tsp paprika

pinch of salt

1 Deseed and chop the bell pepper.

2 Combine the golden raisins, bell pepper, celery, sweetcorn, apple and grapes in a large bowl. Stir in the rice, and shrimp, if using.

3 For the dressing, put the mayonnaise, curry powder, lemon juice, paprika and salt into a small bowl and mix well.

4 Pour the dressing over the salad and gently mix until evenly coated.

5 Line the serving plate with cos lettuce leaves and spoon on the salad. Sprinkle over the paprika and serve.

COOK'S TIP

Mayonnaise can be bought in varying thicknesses, from the type that you spoon out of the jar to the pouring variety. If you need to thin down mayonnaise for a dressing, simply add water little by little until the desired consistency is reached.

hot salad

serves four

½ medium-sized cauliflower

1 green bell pepper

1 red bell pepper

½ cucumber

4 carrots

2 tbsp butter

salt and pepper

crusty bread, rolls or garlic bread,
   to serve

DRESSING

3 tbsp olive oil

1 tbsp white wine vinegar

1 tbsp light soy sauce

1 tsp superfine sugar

salt and pepper

1 Cut the cauliflower into small florets, using a sharp knife. Seed the bell peppers and cut the flesh into thin slices. Cut the cucumber into thin slices. Thinly slice the carrots lengthwise.

2 Melt the butter in a large, heavy pan. Add the cauliflower florets, bell peppers, cucumber, and carrots and cook over medium heat, stirring constantly, for 5–7 minutes, until tender, but still firm to the bite. Season with salt and pepper. Lower the heat, cover with a lid, and simmer for 3 minutes.

3 Meanwhile, make the dressing. Whisk together all the ingredients until thoroughly combined.

4 Transfer the vegetables to a serving dish, pour over the dressing, toss to mix well, and serve immediately.

COOK'S TIP

You can replace the vegetables in this recipe with any of your choice, such as broccoli, scallions, and zucchini.

pesto risotto-rice salad

serves four–six

3 tbsp extra-virgin olive oil, plus
   extra for drizzling

1 onion, finely chopped

1 cup arborio rice

2 cups boiling water

6 sun-dried tomatoes in oil, drained
   and cut into thin slivers

½ small red onion, very thinly sliced

3 tbsp lemon juice

PESTO

2 oz/55 g fresh basil leaves

2 garlic cloves, finely chopped

2 tbsp pine nuts, lightly toasted

½ cup extra-virgin olive oil

½ cup freshly grated Parmesan cheese

salt and pepper

TO GARNISH

fresh basil leaves

Parmesan shavings

1 To make the pesto, put the basil, garlic, and pine nuts in a food processor and process for 30 seconds. With the motor running, gradually add the olive oil through the feeder tube until a smooth paste forms. Add the cheese and pulse until blended, but still with texture. Scrape into a small bowl and season to taste.

2 Heat 1 tablespoon of the oil in a pan and cook the chopped onion until soft. Stir in the rice and cook, stirring occasionally, for 2 minutes. Stir in the water and season. Cover and simmer for 20 minutes until the rice is tender and the water absorbed. Cool slightly.

3 Put the sun-dried tomatoes and sliced onion in a bowl, and add the lemon juice and 2 tablespoons of oil. Fork in the hot rice and stir in the pesto. Toss to combine. Adjust the seasoning if necessary. Cover and cool to room temperature.

4 Fork the rice mixture into a shallow serving bowl. Drizzle with some olive oil and garnish with basil leaves and Parmesan shavings. Serve the salad at room temperature, not chilled.

asian lettuce cups

serves four

8 leaves Romaine lettuce, or similar
    firm lettuce leaves

2 carrots

2 celery sticks

3½ oz baby corn

2 scallions

1 cup bean sprouts

2 tbsp chopped roasted peanuts

DRESSING

2 tbsp smooth peanut butter

3 tbsp lime juice

3 tbsp coconut milk

2 tsp soya sauce

1 tsp sugar

1 tsp grated fresh ginger

½ tsp Thai red curry paste

1 Wash and trim the lettuce leaves, leaving them whole. Arrange on a serving plate or on individual plates.

2 Trim the carrots and celery and cut into fine matchsticks. Trim the corn and onions and slice both diagonally. Toss together all the prepared vegetables with the bean sprouts. Divide the salad between the lettuce cups.

3 To make the dressing, place all the ingredients in a screw-top jar and shake well until thoroughly mixed.

4 Spoon the dressing evenly over the salad cups and sprinkle with chopped peanuts. Serve immediately.

COOK'S TIP

Choose leaves with a deep cup shape to hold the salad neatly. If you prefer, Chinese cabbage may be used in place of the Romaine lettuce. To remove the leaves from the whole head without tearing them, cut a thick slice from the base end so the leaves are not attached by their stems, then gently ease away the leafy parts.

pasta salad with nuts & gorgonzola

serves four

8 oz/225 g dried farfalle

2 tbsp walnut oil

4 tbsp safflower oil

2 tbsp balsamic vinegar

salt and pepper

10 oz/280 g mixed salad greens

8 oz/225 g gorgonzola cheese, diced

½ cup walnuts, halved and toasted

VARIATION

Substitute hazelnuts for the walnuts and hazelnut oil for the walnut oil, if you prefer. Replace the farfalle with pennerigate or fusilli.

---

1 Bring a large heavy-bottom pan of lightly salted water to a boil. Add the pasta, return to a boil, and cook for 8–10 minutes, or until tender but still firm to the bite. Drain and refresh in a bowl of cold water. Drain again.

2 Mix the walnut oil, safflower oil, and vinegar together in a measuring cup, whisking well, and season to taste with salt and pepper.

3 Arrange the salad greens in a large serving bowl. Top with the pasta, gorgonzola cheese, and walnuts. Pour the dressing over the salad, toss lightly, and serve.

tomato, artichoke & bean salad

serves four

4 ripe plum tomatoes, cut into wedges

4 oz/115 g baby plum tomatoes, halved

14 oz/400 g canned artichoke hearts, drained

14 oz/400 g canned lima beans, drained and rinsed

2 tbsp corn or peanut oil

4 tbsp Thai sweet chili dipping sauce

juice of ½ lime

pepper

fresh crusty bread, to serve

1 Place all the tomatoes in a large bowl. Cut the drained artichoke hearts in half, then add to the bowl of tomatoes. Add the lima beans and gently stir together.

2 Mix the oil, chili dipping sauce, and lime juice together in a small bowl. Season to taste with pepper and pour over the salad. Toss gently until the salad is coated with the dressing.

3 Cover and let marinate for 1 hour before serving with crusty bread.

VARIATION

Substitute your favorite beans for the lima beans—cannellini or flageolets would be equally good.

tabbouleh

serves four

1 cup bulgur wheat

3 tbsp extra-virgin olive oil

4 tbsp lemon juice

salt and pepper

4 scallions

1 green bell pepper, seeded and sliced

4 tomatoes, chopped

2 tbsp chopped fresh parsley

2 tbsp chopped fresh mint

8 black olives, pitted

fresh mint sprigs, to garnish

COOK'S TIP

The grains of bulgur wheat have been cracked by boiling and so are partially cooked, so all it needs is rehydrating. Don't make this salad too far in advance as it may go soggy.

1 Place the bulgur wheat in a large bowl and add enough cold water to cover. Let stand for 30 minutes, or until the wheat has doubled in size. Drain well and press out as much liquid as possible. Spread out the wheat on paper towels to dry.

2 Place the wheat in a serving bowl. Mix the olive oil and lemon

VARIATION

Use different types of fresh tomatoes—try vine-ripened tomatoes, which have a delicate, sweet flavor, or cherry tomatoes, cut in half.

juice together in a measuring cup and season to taste with salt and pepper. Pour the lemon mixture over the wheat and let marinate for 1 hour.

3 Using a sharp knife, finely chop the scallions, then add to the salad with the green bell pepper, tomatoes, parsley, and mint, and toss lightly to mix. Top the salad with the olives and garnish with fresh mint sprigs, then serve.

Side Salads

Even a simple mixed leaf salad is the perfect accompaniment to so many dishes; grills, casseroles, risottos, and baked pasta, for example, but side salads can offer much more. Carefully chosen, they can complement the flavors and textures of the main course or provide a contrast and balance. Try serving Potato Salad (see page 190) instead of French fries with steak, or Moroccan Couscous Salad (see page 200) with a spicy stew to counteract the heat. Green Bean & Carrot Salad (see page 188) balances the likes of lemony chicken, while Tropical Rice Salad (see page 191) is the perfect partner for barbecued ribs. You could also serve these salads in the French style, by eating them as a palate cleanser before dessert.

feta cheese salad

serves four

1¾ oz/50 g fresh green salad leaves

handful of fresh cilantro leaves

½ cucumber, chopped

4 scallions, finely diced

4 tomatoes, sliced

12 black olives, pitted and sliced

5 oz/140 g feta cheese

CILANTRO DRESSING

4 tbsp extra-virgin olive oil

1 tbsp lime juice

1 tbsp chopped fresh cilantro

salt and pepper

1 Wash and drain the salad leaves, if necessary. Shred the leaves and arrange in the bottom of a large salad bowl. Add the cilantro leaves, cucumber, scallions, tomatoes, and olives.

2 Cut the cheese into thin slices or small chunks, then transfer to the salad bowl. Mix together gently.

3 Put the dressing ingredients into a screw-top jar, screw on the lid tightly, and shake well until thoroughly combined. Drizzle the dressing over the salad and serve immediately.

COOK'S TIP

If chilled, allow a good thirty minutes for the feta cheese to come to room temperature to fully enjoy its rich, tangy flavor and creamy texture.

carrot, cabbage & mixed fruit salad

serves four

7 oz/200 g raw carrots

7 oz/200 g raw white cabbage

3½ oz/100 g sprouting beans

1¾ oz/50 g alfalfa sprouts

generous ⅓ cup golden raisins

generous ⅓ cup raisins

1 tbsp lemon juice

1 Trim and peel the carrots, then grate them into a large salad bowl. Trim the white cabbage, then shred it finely. Transfer it to a large strainer and rinse under cold running water. Drain well, then add it to the carrots.

2 Put the sprouting beans and alfalfa into the strainer and rinse well, then drain and add to the salad. Rinse and drain all the fruit and then add it to the bowl. Pour in the lemon juice, toss the salad in it, and serve.

COOK'S TIP
Try adding some small nuts or seeds to this dish, to give it a bit of extra crunch.

beet, apple & celery salad

serves four

2 apples

2 large or 4 small cooked beets

2 celery stalks

scant ½ cup plain yogurt

1 tbsp lemon juice

1 Wash and core the apples, but leave the skin on. Grate them into a large salad bowl.

2 Grate the beets, then add them to the bowl with the apples. Wash and trim the celery stalks, cut them into small pieces, then add them to the salad.

3 Add the yogurt and lemon juice, mix until all the ingredients are thoroughly combined, then serve.

COOK'S TIP

To cook beets in the oven, wrap individually in thick, quality kitchen foil. Bake at 375°F/190°C for about 1 to 1¼ hours for medium-sized beet, or until tender. To microwave, place one pound whole beets in a covered dish with ¼ cup water and cook for 10 to 11 minutes or until tender. Let stand, covered, for at least 5 minutes.

avocado, corn & walnut salad

serves four

12 oz/350 g canned corn kernels

2¾ oz/75 g walnuts, chopped

2 large, ripe avocados

6 tbsp lemon juice

6 tbsp sour cream

VARIATION

To alter the overall taste of this dish, replace the sour cream with crème frâiche or thick, creamy, Greek-style yogurt.

1 Drain the corn kernels, then put them into a large salad bowl. Add the walnuts and mix until well combined.

2 Peel and pit the avocados, brush them with some of the lemon juice to prevent discoloration, then add them to the salad.

3 In a separate bowl, mix the remaining lemon juice with the sour cream until a smooth consistency is reached. Add more lemon juice or cream if necessary. Add the lemon cream to the salad, stir it in, and serve.

fava beans with mozzarella & basil

serves four

1 lb/450 g fava beans (shelled
  weight)

4 tbsp extra-virgin olive oil

1 tbsp lime juice

1 tbsp finely chopped fresh basil

2¼ oz/60 g firm mozzarella

GARNISH

finely chopped fresh mint

wedges of lime

COOK'S TIP

When planning to cook this
dish make sure that you leave
enough time for the beans
to cool before dressing and
adding the mozzarella.

1 Bring a pan of water to a boil,
then add the fava beans and cook
for 2 minutes. Drain well and let cool.

2 In a separate bowl, mix together
the olive oil, lime juice, and
chopped basil.

3 When the beans are cool, transfer
them to a large salad bowl. Pour
over the oil dressing and mix until well
combined. Cut the mozzarella into
cubes and stir them gently into the
salad. Garnish with chopped fresh mint
and lime wedges and serve.

moorish zucchini salad

serves four–six

1lb 2 oz/500 g small zucchini

about 4 tbsp olive oil

1 large garlic clove, halved

⅓ cup pine nuts

⅓ cup raisins

3 tbsp finely chopped fresh mint
leaves (not spearmint
or peppermint)

about 2 tbsp lemon juice, or to taste

salt and pepper

VARIATION

For a more robust flavor, chop 4 drained anchovy fillets in oil and add in Step 2.

COOK'S TIP

This salad is best made with young, tender zucchini no more than 1 inch/2.5 cm thick. If using older, larger zucchini, cut them in half or fourths lengthwise first, then slice thinly.

1 Slice the zucchini thinly (see Cook's Tip). Heat the oil in a large skillet over medium heat. Add the garlic and let it cook until golden to flavor the oil, then remove and discard. Add the zucchini and cook, stirring, until just tender. Immediately remove from the skillet and transfer to a large serving bowl.

2 Add the pine nuts, raisins, mint, lemon juice, and salt and pepper to taste, and stir. Taste, and add more olive oil, lemon juice, and seasoning, if necessary.

3 Let the salad cool completely. Cover and chill for at least 3½ hours. Remove from the refrigerator 10 minutes before serving.

spicy tomato salad

serves four

4 large ripe tomatoes

1 oz/25 g fresh basil

1 small red chili

1 garlic clove

4 tbsp extra-virgin olive oil

1 tbsp lemon juice

2 tbsp balsamic vinegar

salt and pepper

GARNISH

sprigs of fresh basil

wedges of lemon

fresh crusty bread, to serve

1 Bring a pot of water to a boil. Put the tomatoes into a heatproof bowl, then pour over enough boiling water to cover them. Let them soak for 2–4 minutes, then lift them out of the water and let cool slightly.

2 When the tomatoes are cool enough to handle, gently pierce the

skins with the point of a knife. You should now find the skins easy to remove. Discard the skins, then chop the tomatoes and place them in a large salad bowl.

3 Seed and finely chop the chili, then chop the garlic. Wash and finely chop the basil, then add it to the tomatoes with the chili and the garlic.

4 In a separate bowl, mix together the oil, lemon juice, and balsamic vinegar, then season with salt and pepper. Pour the mixture over the salad and toss together well. Garnish with basil sprigs and lemon wedges, and serve with fresh crusty bread.

mixed cabbage coleslaw with fruit

COOK'S TIP

Different cabbage varieties are available throughout the year. Cabbage is low in fat and has a good dietary fiber and iron content.

1 Wash and shred the white and red cabbage. Grate the carrots, and finely chop the onion. Put all the prepared vegetables into a large salad bowl, then wash the fruit and add to the bowl.

2 In a separate bowl, mix together the mayonnaise and lemon juice, season with salt and pepper, and pour over the salad. Mix all the ingredients together until well combined. Serve at once, or cover with plastic wrap and refrigerate until ready to use.

sweet potato & bean salad

serves four

1 sweet potato

4 baby carrots, halved

4 tomatoes

4 celery stalks, chopped

8 oz/225 g canned cranberry beans,
   drained and rinsed

4 oz/115 g mixed salad greens,
   such as frisée, arugula, radicchio
   and oak leaf lettuce

1 tbsp golden raisins

4 scallions, finely chopped

½ cup honey and yogurt dressing
   (see Cook's Tip)

1 Peel and dice the sweet potato. Bring a pan of water to a boil over medium heat. Add the sweet potato and cook for 10 minutes, until tender. Drain the potato, transfer to a bowl, and set aside.

2 Cook the carrots in a separate pan of boiling water for 1 minute. Drain thoroughly and add to the sweet potato. Cut the tops off the tomatoes and scoop out the seeds. Chop the flesh and add to the bowl with the celery and beans. Mix well.

3 Line a large serving bowl with the mixed salad greens. Spoon the sweet potato and bean mixture on top, then sprinkle with the golden raisins and scallions. Spoon over the dressing and serve immediately.

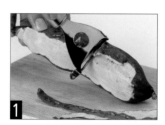

COOK'S TIP

For a quick and easy lowfat dressing, put one tablespoon of clear honey in a bowl, add 6 tablespoons of lowfat natural yogurt and beat until blended. Season to taste.

pasta salad with curry dressing

serves four

4 oz/115 g dried farfalle

4–5 large lettuce leaves

1 green bell pepper, seeded and
  chopped

1 red bell pepper, seeded and
  chopped

2 tbsp chopped fresh chives

4 oz/115 g white mushrooms,
  chopped

DRESSING

2 tsp curry powder

1 tbsp superfine sugar

½ cup corn oil

¼ cup white wine vinegar

1 tbsp light cream

VARIATION

Replace the farfalle with other
pasta shapes such as penne,
fusilli, or conchiglie and use
cremini mushrooms instead of
the white ones, if you prefer.

1 Bring a large heavy-bottom pan
of lightly salted water to a boil.
Add the pasta, return to a boil, and
cook for 8–10 minutes, or until tender
but still firm to the bite. Drain, rinse in
a bowl of cold water, and drain again.

2 Line a large bowl with the lettuce
leaves and tip in the pasta. Add
the green and red bell peppers, chives,
and mushrooms.

3 To make the dressing, place the
curry powder and sugar in a small
bowl and gradually stir in the oil, vinegar,
and cream. Whisk well and pour the
dressing over the salad. Toss and serve.

green bean & carrot salad

12 oz/350 g green beans

8 oz/225 g carrots

1 red bell pepper

1 red onion

DRESSING

2 tbsp extra-virgin olive oil

1 tbsp red wine vinegar

2 tsp sun-dried tomato paste

¼ tsp superfine sugar

salt and pepper

COOK'S TIP

Use canned beans if fresh ones are unavailable. Rinse off the salty liquid and drain well. There is no need to blanch canned beans.

1 Blanch the beans in boiling water for 4 minutes, until just tender. Drain the beans and rinse them under cold running water until they are cool. Drain again thoroughly. Transfer the beans to a large salad bowl.

2 Cut the carrots into thin sticks, using a mandolin if you have one. Halve and seed the bell pepper and cut the flesh into thin strips. Cut the red onion into thin slices.

3 Add the carrot, bell pepper, and onion to the beans and toss to mix.

4 To make the dressing, place the olive oil, wine vinegar, sun-dried tomato paste, sugar, and salt and pepper to taste in a small screw-top jar and shake well. Pour the dressing over the vegetables and serve immediately, or let chill in the refrigerator until required.

potato salad

1 lb 9 oz/700 g tiny new potatoes

8 scallions

1 hard-cooked egg (optional)

1 cup mayonnaise

1 tsp paprika

salt and pepper

TO GARNISH

2 tbsp snipped fresh chives

pinch of paprika

1 Bring a large pan of lightly salted water to a boil. Add the potatoes and cook for 10–15 minutes, or until just tender.

2 Drain the potatoes and rinse them under cold running water until completely cold. Drain again. Transfer the potatoes to a bowl and reserve until required.

3 Using a sharp knife, slice the scallions thinly on the diagonal. Chop the hard-cooked egg, if using.

4 Mix the mayonnaise, paprika, and salt and pepper to taste together

COOK'S TIP

Add cubes of cheese to the potato salad, if liked. To make a lighter dressing, use a mixture of half mayonnaise and half plain yogurt.

in a bowl. Pour the mixture over the potatoes. Add the scallions and egg, if using, to the potatoes and toss together.

5 Transfer the potato salad to a serving bowl and sprinkle with snipped chives and a pinch of paprika. Cover and let chill in the refrigerator until required.

tropical rice salad

serves four

½ cup long-grain rice

salt and pepper

4 scallions

8 oz/225 g canned pineapple pieces
in natural juice

7 oz/200 g canned corn, drained

2 red bell peppers, seeded and
diced

3 tbsp golden raisins

DRESSING

1 tbsp peanut oil

1 tbsp hazelnut oil

1 tbsp light soy sauce

1 garlic clove, finely chopped

1 tsp chopped fresh gingerroot

2 Using a sharp knife, finely chop the scallions. Drain the pineapple pieces, reserving the juice in a measuring cup. Add the pineapple pieces, corn, red bell peppers, chopped scallions, and golden raisins to the rice and mix lightly.

3 Add all the dressing ingredients to the reserved pineapple juice, whisking well, and season to taste with salt and pepper. Pour the dressing over the salad and toss until the salad is thoroughly coated. Serve immediately.

1 Cook the rice in a large pan of lightly salted boiling water for 15 minutes, or until tender. Drain thoroughly and rinse under cold running water. Place the rice in a large serving bowl.

roast potato salad

serves four

1 lb/450 g new potatoes

6 tbsp olive oil

1 garlic clove, crushed

salt and pepper

1 tbsp red wine vinegar

1 tsp white sugar

3 tbsp chopped fresh parsley leaves

12 cherry tomatoes, halved

½ cucumber, diced and unpeeled

1 orange bell pepper, cored,
    seeded, and diced

4 scallions, sliced thinly

1 Preheat the oven to 400°F/200°C. Spread out the potatoes in a large roasting pan. Combine 4 tablespoons of the olive oil with the garlic, salt, and pepper, and drizzle it over the potatoes. Transfer to the preheated oven and roast for about 45 minutes, turning once or twice during cooking, until they are tender and golden brown.

2 Meanwhile, make a dressing by combining the remaining oil with the vinegar, sugar, and parsley. Season to taste.

3 When the potatoes are cooked, remove them from the oven, let cool completely, and put into a salad bowl. Add the tomatoes, cucumber, orange bell pepper, and scallions and toss together.

4 Drizzle the dressing over the salad and toss again. Cover with plastic wrap and chill in the refrigerator before serving.

COOK'S TIP

Make sure you coat the potatoes thoroughly in oil so that when you turn them during cooking each side will brown.

chickpea salad

serves four

1½ cups canned chickpeas

4 carrots

1 bunch of scallions

1 cucumber

½ tsp salt

½ tsp pepper

3 tbsp lemon juice

1 red bell pepper, seeded and
   thinly sliced

1 Drain the chickpeas and place them in a large salad bowl.

2 Using a sharp knife, peel and slice the carrots. Cut the scallions into thin strips. Slice the cucumber, then cut into thick fourths. Add the carrots, scallions, and cucumber to the chickpeas and mix.

3 Stir in the salt and pepper and sprinkle with the lemon juice.

4 Gently toss the salad ingredients together using 2 serving spoons.

5 Using a sharp knife, slice the red bell pepper thinly.

6 Arrange the slices of red bell pepper on top of the chickpea salad. Serve the salad immediately or let chill in the refrigerator and serve when required.

COOK'S TIP

Using canned chickpeas rather than the dried ones speeds up the cooking time.

warm potatoes with pesto

serves four

1 lb/450 g small new potatoes

3 tsp pesto sauce

salt and pepper

⅓ cup freshly grated Parmesan
  cheese

1 Cook the potatoes in salted boiling water for about 15 minutes, or until tender. Drain, put in a salad bowl, and let cool slightly.

2 Add the pesto, salt, and pepper to the potatoes and toss together. Sprinkle with the Parmesan cheese and serve warm.

COOK'S TIP

This dish is so quick and
easy to make if you use
prepreared pesto.

VARIATION

Dice some bacon, fry in a
small amount of olive oil until
crispy and then sprinkle on top
of the warm salad.

kachumbers

each serves six

TOMATO, ONION & CUCUMBER
KACHUMBER

3 ripe tomatoes

¼ cucumber, peeled

1 small onion, quartered

1 tsp lime juice

2 green chilies, deseeded and
chopped (optional)

MANGO KACHUMBER

½ mango, peeled and chopped

1 small onion, chopped

1 tbsp chopped fresh cilantro

2 tomatoes, chopped

RADISH KACHUMBER

8 large radishes, sliced

½ cucumber, peeled and chopped

1 small onion, chopped

1 tbsp chopped fresh cilantro

1 tbsp oil

1 tbsp vinegar

1 To make the tomato, onion, and cucumber kachumber, peel the tomatoes. Make a small cross in the top of each one with a pointed knife, place in a bowl, and cover with boiling water. Leave for 1 minute before draining. The skins will slip off easily. Cut the tomatoes into quarters and cut each quarter in half. The seeds can be removed at this stage, if you prefer. Cut the cucumber lengthwise into quarters. Remove the seeds and cut the flesh into cubes. Cut each onion quarter into slices. Combine all the ingredients in a bowl and sprinkle with the lime juice. Add the chilies, if using, and serve.

2 To make the mango kachumber, mix all the ingredients together and serve.

3 To make the radish kachumber, combine all the ingredients in a bowl and serve.

mushroom salad

serves four

5½ oz/150 g firm white mushrooms

4 tbsp virgin olive oil

1 tbsp lemon juice

5 canned anchovy fillets, drained
and chopped

1 tbsp fresh marjoram

salt and pepper

1 Gently wipe each mushroom with a damp cloth or damp paper towels in order to remove any dirt.

2 Slice the mushrooms thinly, using a sharp knife and place in a bowl.

3 To make the dressing, whisk together the olive oil and lemon juice.

4 Pour the dressing mixture over the mushrooms. Toss together so that the mushrooms are completely coated with the lemon juice and oil.

5 Stir the chopped anchovy fillets into the mushrooms. Season the mixture with pepper to taste and garnish with the fresh marjoram.

6 Set the mushroom salad aside at room temperature for about 5 minutes before serving to allow all the flavors to be absorbed.

7 Season the mushroom salad with a little salt (see Cook's Tip) and then serve immediately.

COOK'S TIP

Do not season the mushroom salad with salt until the very last minute as it will cause the mushrooms to blacken and the juices to leak. The result will not be so tasty, as the full flavors won't be absorbed and it will also look very unattractive.

potato & arugula salad

serves four

1 lb 5 oz/600 g potatoes, unpeeled
and sliced

2 green dessert apples, diced

1 tsp lemon juice

¼ cup walnut pieces

4 oz/115 g goat cheese, cubed

5 oz arugula leaves

salt and pepper

DRESSING

2 tbsp olive oil

1 tbsp red wine vinegar

1 tsp honey

1 tsp fennel seeds

COOK'S TIP

Serve this salad immediately
to prevent the apple from
discoloring. Alternatively, prepare
all of the other ingredients in
advance and add the apple at
the last minute.

1 Cook the potatoes in a pan of
boiling water for 15 minutes until
tender. Drain and let cool. Transfer the
cooled potatoes to a serving bowl.

2 Toss the diced apples in the
lemon juice, then drain and stir
them into the cold potatoes.

3 Add the walnut pieces, cheese
cubes, and arugula leaves, then
toss the ingredients together to mix.

4 In a small bowl, whisk all of the
dressing ingredients together and
then pour the dressing over the salad.
Season to taste and serve immediately.

moroccan couscous salad

serves four

1⅓ cups couscous

1 cinnamon stick, about 2 inches/5 cm

2 tsp coriander seeds

1 tsp cumin seeds

2 tbsp olive oil

1 small onion, finely chopped

2 garlic cloves, finely chopped

½ tsp ground turmeric

pinch of cayenne pepper

1 tbsp lemon juice

⅓ cup golden raisins

3 ripe plum tomatoes, chopped

3 oz/85 g cucumber, chopped

4 scallions, sliced

7 oz/200 g can tuna in olive oil,
    drained and flaked

3 tbsp chopped fresh cilantro

salt and pepper

COOK'S TIP

The tuna should be
canned in olive oil and
not water as this will alter the
taste of the dish.

1 Cook the couscous according to the packet instructions, omitting any butter recommended. Transfer to a large bowl and set aside.

2 Heat a small skillet and add the cinnamon stick, coriander seeds, and cumin seeds. Cook over high heat until the seeds begin to pop and smell fragrant. Remove from the heat and grind to a fine powder with a pestle and mortar or in a spice grinder. Set aside.

3 Heat the oil in a clean skillet and add the onion. Cook over low heat for 7–8 minutes until softened and lightly browned. Add the garlic and cook for a further minute. Stir in the roasted and ground spices, turmeric, and cayenne and cook for a further minute. Remove from the heat and stir in the lemon juice. Add this mixture to the couscous and mix well together, ensuring that all of the grains are well coated.

4 Add the golden raisins, tomatoes, cucumber, scallions, tuna, and chopped cilantro. Season with salt and pepper to taste and mix together well. Allow the salad to cool completely and serve at room temperature.

eggplant salad

serves four

1 lb 2 oz/500 g eggplants

4 tbsp salt

1 tbsp olive oil

1 large onion, chopped

1 garlic clove, crushed

⅔ cup vegetable stock

14 oz/400 g can chopped tomatoes

2 tbsp tomato paste

1 tsp ground cinnamon

2 tsp superfine sugar

1 tbsp chopped fresh cilantro

1 tbsp lemon juice

15 oz/425 g can garbanzo beans,
     drained

pepper

fresh cilantro sprigs to garnish

TO SERVE

warm pitas

lemon wedges

COOK'S TIP

The consistency of this salad
should be fairly mushy,
but not watery. If it looks as if
it is still holding too much
liquid then extend the simmering
time slightly.

1 Cut the eggplants into ½ inch/
1 cm thick slices and then dice.
Layer them in a bowl, sprinkling well
with salt as you go. Set aside for 30
minutes for the bitter juices to drain out.

2 Transfer to a colander and rinse
well under cold running water to
remove the salt. Drain thoroughly and
pat dry with paper towels.

3 Heat the oil in a large nonstick
skillet, add the onion and garlic,
and cook over low heat, stirring
occasionally, for 2–3 minutes until
slightly softened.

4 Pour in the stock and bring to a
boil. Add the eggplants, canned
tomatoes, tomato paste, cinnamon,
sugar, and pepper. Mix well and simmer
gently, uncovered, for 20 minutes until
softened. Remove from the heat and
set aside to cool completely.

5 Stir in the fresh cilantro, lemon
juice, and garbanzo beans, cover,
and chill for 1 hour.

6 Garnish with cilantro sprigs and
serve with warmed pitas and
lemon wedges.

mexican potato salad

serves four

2 lb 12 oz/1.25 kg waxy potatoes, sliced

1 ripe avocado

1 tsp olive oil

1 tsp lemon juice

1 garlic clove, crushed

1 onion, chopped

2 large tomatoes, sliced

1 green chili, chopped

1 yellow bell pepper, seeded and sliced

2 tbsp chopped fresh cilantro

salt and pepper

lemon wedges, to garnish

COOK'S TIP

You can omit the green chili from this salad if you do not like hot dishes.

1 Cook the potato slices in a pan of boiling water for 10–15 minutes, or until tender. Drain and let cool.

2 Meanwhile, cut the avocado in half and remove the pit. Mash the avocado flesh with a fork (you could also scoop the avocado flesh from the 2 halves using a spoon and then mash it).

3 Add the olive oil, lemon juice, garlic, and chopped onion to the avocado flesh and stir to mix. Cover the bowl with plastic wrap, to minimize discoloration, and set aside.

4 Mix the tomatoes, chili, and yellow bell pepper together and transfer to a salad bowl with the potato slices.

5 Arrange the avocado mixture on top of the salad and sprinkle with the chopped fresh cilantro. Season to taste with salt and pepper and serve garnished with lemon wedges.

green sesame salad

serves four

4½ oz/125 g/2 cups bean sprouts

1½ tbsp chopped fresh cilantro

3 tbsp fresh lime juice

½ tsp mild chili powder

1 tsp sugar

½ tsp salt

3 celery sticks

1 large green bell pepper, deseeded

1 large Granny Smith apple

2 tbsp toasted sesame seeds,
   to garnish

1 Rinse the bean sprouts and drain thoroughly.

2 Pick over the bean sprouts, removing any that seem a little brown or limp – it is essential that they are fresh and crunchy for this recipe.

3 To make the dressing, combine the cilantro, lime juice, chili powder, sugar and salt in a small bowl and mix thoroughly.

4 Using a sharp knife, cut the celery into 2.5 cm/1 inch pieces. Cut the bell pepper into small pieces and the Granny Smith apple into small chunks.

5 Place the chopped celery, bell pepper and apple into a large mixing bowl and stir gently to mix.

6 Just before serving, pour the dressing over the salad, tossing well to mix.

7 Garnish the green sesame salad with the toasted sesame seeds and serve with rice or noodle dishes.

broccoli & almond salad

serves four

1 lb/450 g small broccoli florets

1¾ oz/50 g baby corn cobs, halved, lengthways

1 red bell pepper, seeded and cut into thin strips

1¾ oz/50 g blanched almonds

DRESSING

1 tbsp sesame seeds

1 tbsp peanut oil

2 garlic cloves, crushed

2 tbsp light soy sauce

1 tbsp clear honey

2 tsp lemon juice

pepper

lemon zest, to garnish (optional)

lightly browned and are giving off a delicious aroma.

1 Blanch the broccoli and baby corn cobs in boiling water for 5 minutes. Drain well, rinse and drain again.

2 Transfer the broccoli and baby corn cobs to a large mixing bowl and add the bell pepper and almonds.

3 To make the dressing, heat a wok and add the sesame seeds. Dry-fry, stirring constantly, for about 1 minute, or until the sesame seeds are

4 Mix the peanut oil, garlic, soy sauce, honey, lemon juice, and pepper to taste. Add the sesame seeds and mix well.

5 Pour the dressing over the salad, cover and set aside in the refrigerator for a minimum of 4 hours and preferably overnight.

6 Garnish the salad with lemon zest (if using) and serve.

spinach & garlic salad

serves four

12 garlic cloves

4 tbsp olive oil

1 lb/450 g baby spinach leaves

½ cup chopped walnuts or pine nuts

2 tbsp lemon juice

salt and ground black pepper

VARIATION

Substitute young sorrel leaves
for the spinach for a delicious
lemony flavor.

---

1 Do not peel the garlic. Place the cloves in an ovenproof dish, add 2 tbsp of the olive oil, and toss well to coat. Roast in a preheated oven, 375°F/ 190°C, for 15 minutes.

2 Transfer the garlic and oil to a salad bowl. Add the spinach, walnuts or pine nuts, lemon juice, and remaining oil. Toss well to coat and season to taste with salt and pepper.

3 Serve the salad immediately while the garlic is still warm—the diners squeeze the softened garlic out of the skins at the table.

cucumber salad

serves four

1 cucumber

1 tsp salt

1 small red onion

1 garlic clove, crushed

½ tsp chili paste

2 tsp Thai fish sauce

1 tbsp lime juice

1 tsp sesame oil

COOK'S TIP

Once the salad is made, it can be chilled with the dressing for about 1–2 hours, but is best eaten on the day of making.

1 Trim the cucumber and coarsely grate the flesh. Place it in a strainer over a bowl, sprinkle with the salt, and set aside to drain for about 20 minutes. Discard the liquid and rinse the cucumber.

2 Peel the onion and chop finely, then add it to the cucumber. Toss to mix. Spoon the mixture into 4 individual bowls or a large serving bowl.

3 Combine the garlic, chili paste, fish sauce, lime juice, and sesame oil, then spoon the dressing over the salad. Cover the salad tightly with plastic wrap and chill in the refrigerator before serving.

thai green salad

serves four–six

1 small head Romaine lettuce

1 bunch scallions

1½ cucumber

4 tbsp coarsely shredded fresh
coconut, toasted

DRESSING

4 tbsp lime juice

2 tbsp Thai fish sauce

1 small bird's eye chili, finely chopped

1 tsp sugar

1 garlic clove, crushed

2 tbsp chopped fresh cilantro

1 tbsp chopped fresh mint

1 Tear or roughly shred the lettuce leaves and place in a large salad bowl.

2 Trim and thinly slice the scallions diagonally and add to the salad bowl.

3 Use a vegetable peeler to shave thin slices along the length of the cucumber and add to the salad bowl.

4 Place all the ingredients for the dressing in a screw-top jar and shake well to mix thoroughly.

COOK'S TIP

To transport this salad easily pack the leaves into a large plastic container then nestle the screw-top jar of dressing in the center. Cover with a lid or plastic wrap. This way, the salad stays crisp and even if the dressing leaks during transit, there's no nasty mess.

5 Pour the dressing over the salad and toss well to coat the leaves evenly. Scatter the coconut over the salad and toss in lightly just before serving.

bamboo shoot salad

serves four

2 shallots

2 garlic cloves

2 tbsp Thai fish sauce

3 tbsp lime juice

½ tsp dried chili flakes

1 tsp granulated sugar

1 tbsp round grain rice

2 tsp sesame seeds

12 oz can bamboo shoots, drained

2 scallions, chopped

shredded Chinese cabbage or
    lettuce, to serve

mint leaves, to garnish

1 Place the whole shallots and garlic under a medium-hot broiler and broil until charred on the outside and tender inside. Remove the skins and place the flesh in a mortar and pestle. Crush to a smooth paste.

2 Mix the paste with the fish sauce, lime juice, chili flakes, and sugar.

3 Place the rice and sesame seeds in a heavy-based frying pan over the heat and cook to a rich golden brown, shaking the pan to brown evenly. Remove from the heat and crush lightly in a mortar and pestle.

4 Use a sharp knife to shred the bamboo shoots into fine matchsticks. Stir in the shallot and garlic dressing, tossing well to coat evenly. Stir in the toasted rice and sesame, then the scallions.

5 Pile the salad onto a serving dish and surround with shredded Chinese cabbage. Garnish with mint leaves and serve.

211

Fruit Salads

There can be few more delightful, refreshing, and, indeed, healthy ways to end a meal than with a fruit salad. With a touch of sweetness, pretty colors, luscious flavors, and a delicate texture, they appeal to everyone, young and old. The guiding rule when combining fruits is to keep like with like, so put tropical fruits together, combine Mediterranean fruits, and mix and match home-grown fruits. The recipes in this chapter do exactly that with some clever and original twists. Fruit Salad with Ginger Syrup (see page 242) is a taste sensation, while Pear & Roquefort Salad (see page 230) is guaranteed to delight gourmet guests. Broiled Fruit Platter (see page 249) is a lovely surprise and, although Italians have been sprinkling strawberries with top-quality vinegar for years, Balsamic Strawberries (see page 252) will be a revelation to anyone who has never tried them before.

tropical fruit salad

6 tbsp superfine sugar

1¾ cups water

½ tsp ground allspice

grated rind of ½ lemon

1 papaya

1 mango

1 pineapple

4 oranges, peeled and cut into
  segments

4½ oz/125 g strawberries, hulled
  and quartered

light or heavy cream, to serve
  (optional)

1 Put the sugar, water, allspice, and lemon rind into a pan. Bring to a boil, stirring continuously, then continue to boil for 1 minute. Remove from the heat and let cool to room temperature. Transfer to a pitcher or bowl, cover with plastic wrap, and chill in the refrigerator for at least 1 hour.

2 Peel and halve the papaya and remove the seeds. Cut the flesh into small chunks or slices, and put into a large bowl. Cut the mango twice lengthwise, close to the stone. Remove

and discard the stone. Peel and cut the flesh into small chunks or slices, and add to the bowl. Cut off the top and bottom of the pineapple and remove the hard skin. Cut the pineapple in half lengthwise, then into quarters, and remove the tough core. Cut the remaining flesh into small pieces and add to the bowl. Add the orange segments and strawberries. Pour over the chilled syrup, cover with plastic wrap, and chill until required. Serve with light or heavy cream, if using.

> **COOK'S TIP**
>
> It is important that you remove the salad from the refrigerator a little while before serving so that the fruit is not too chilled to eat comfortably.

fruit packages

serves four

unsalted butter, for greasing

2 apples

2 bananas

2 oranges

2 tbsp superfine sugar

2 tbsp orange liqueur or orange juice

2 tbsp slivered almonds

COOK'S TIP

Be careful when opening up the packages after cooking as they will be extremely hot. It is best if the packages are left to cool slightly before serving.

VARIATION

Use other fruits, including hulled strawberries, slices of melon, mango and papaya, mandarin segments, and pear chunks, if you prefer.

1 Preheat the oven to 475°F/240°C. Cut 4 large squares of foil and lightly grease with butter. Quarter and core the apples (but do not peel), then slice. Peel and slice the bananas. Peel the oranges, taking care to remove all the pith, then cut into segments and discard the membranes.

2 Place all the fruit in a large bowl and sprinkle the sugar over it. Add the orange liqueur and sprinkle with the almonds. Mix well.

3 Divide the fruit between the pieces of foil and wrap securely into neat packages. Place the packages on a large baking sheet and bake in the preheated oven for 10 minutes. Transfer to serving plates, open up the packages slightly, and serve.

fig & watermelon salad

1 watermelon, weighing about
   3 lb 5 oz/1.5 kg

¾ cup seeded black grapes

4 figs

1 lime

grated rind and juice of 1 orange

1 tbsp maple syrup

2 tbsp honey

4 fresh mint sprigs, to decorate
   (optional)

1 Cut the watermelon into quarters and scoop out and discard the seeds. Cut the flesh away from the rind, then chop the flesh into 1-inch/2.5-cm cubes. Place the watermelon cubes in a bowl with the grapes. Cut each fig lengthwise into 8 wedges and add to the bowl.

VARIATION

Add 2 pieces of chopped preserved ginger to the fruit in Step 1 and replace 1 tablespoon of ginger syrup from the jar for the maple syrup.

2 Grate the lime rind and mix it with the orange rind and juice, maple syrup, and honey in a small pan. Bring to a boil over low heat. Pour the mixture over the fruit and stir. Let cool. Stir again, cover, and let chill in the refrigerator for at least 1 hour, stirring occasionally.

3 To serve, divide the fruit salad equally between 4 glass dishes and decorate with a fresh mint sprig, if you like.

melon & kiwifruit bowl

serves two

1 small charentais, cantaloupe,
   or galia melon

2 kiwifruit

1 Cut the melon into quarters and remove and discard the seeds. Remove the melon flesh from the skin with a sharp knife and cut into chunks. If you have a melon baller, scoop out as much of the melon flesh as possible and place in a bowl.

2 Peel the kiwifruit and cut the flesh into slices. Add to the melon, and gently mix together. Cover and let chill until required or divide between 2 serving dishes and serve at once.

VARIATION

This dessert is perfect in its simplicity, but it is fun to experiment with toppings such as ice cream, sorbet, cream, or a variety of flavored syrups.

grapefruit & cheese salad

serves four

½ Romaine lettuce

½ oak leaf lettuce

2 pink grapefruit

2 ripe avocados

6 oz/175 g dolcelatte cheese,
    thinly sliced

fresh basil sprigs, to garnish

DRESSING

4 tbsp olive oil

1 tbsp white wine vinegar

salt and pepper

1 Arrange the lettuce leaves on 4 serving plates or in a salad bowl.

2 Remove the peel and pith from the grapefruit with a sharp serrated knife, catching the grapefruit juice in a bowl.

3 Segment the grapefruit by cutting down each side of the membrane. Remove all the membrane. Arrange the segments on the serving plates.

4 Peel, pit, and slice the avocados, dipping them in the grapefruit juice to prevent discoloration. Arrange

the slices on the salad with the dolcelatte cheese.

5 To make the dressing, combine any remaining grapefruit juice with the olive oil and wine vinegar. Season with salt and pepper to taste, mixing thoroughly to combine.

6 Drizzle the dressing over the salads. Garnish with fresh basil leaves and serve immediately.

COOK'S TIP

Pink grapefruit segments make a very attractive color combination with the avocados, but ordinary grapefruit will work just as well. To help avocados to ripen, keep them at room temperature in a brown paper bag.

sweet & sour fruit

serves four

14 oz/400 g can mixed fruit cocktail

14 oz/400 g can guavas

2 large bananas

3 apples (optional)

1 tsp ground black pepper

1 tsp salt

½ tsp ground ginger

2 tbsp lemon juice

fresh mint leaves, to garnish

1 Drain the can of mixed fruit cocktail and place the fruit in a large, deep mixing bowl.

2 Mix the the drained fruit cocktail with the guavas and their syrup so that the fruit is well coated.

3 Peel the bananas and cut them into thick slices.

4 Peel and core the apples, if using, and cut them into dice.

5 Add the fresh fruit to the bowl containing the canned fruit and mix thoroughly together.

6 Add the ground black pepper, salt, and ginger and stir to mix. Add the lemon juice to prevent the banana and apple from turning brown and mix again.

7 Serve the sweet and sour fruit as a snack, garnished with a few fresh mint leaves.

COOK'S TIP

Guavas are tropical fruits with a powerful, exotic smell. You may find fresh guavas in specialist shops and large supermarkets, but the canned variety is more widely available. Surprisingly, they have a higher vitamin C content than many citrus fruits.

melon and mango salad

serves four

1 cantaloupe melon
2 oz/55 g black grapes, halved and
    seeded
2 oz/55 g green grapes
1 large mango
1 bunch of watercress, trimmed
iceberg lettuce leaves, shredded
2 tbsp olive oil
1 tbsp apple vinegar
1 passion fruit
salt and pepper
DRESSING
⅔ cup lowfat plain yogurt
1 tbsp honey
1 tsp grated fresh ginger root

1 To make the dressing, for the melon, whisk together the yogurt, honey, and ginger in a small bowl.

2 Halve the melon, scoop out the seeds with a spoon, and discard. Slice, peel, and dice the flesh. Place in a bowl with the grapes.

3 Slice the mango on each side of its large flat pit. On each mango half, slash the flesh into a criss-cross pattern down to, but not through the skin. Push the skin from underneath to turn the mango halves inside out. Now remove the flesh and add to the melon mixture.

4 Arrange the watercress and lettuce leaves on 4 serving plates.

5 Make the dressing for the salad leaves by whisking together the

olive oil and vinegar with a little salt and pepper. Drizzle over the salad greens.

6 Divide the melon mixture among the 4 plates and spoon the yogurt dressing over it.

7 Scoop the seeds out of the passion fruit and sprinkle them over the salads. Serve immediately or chill in the refrigerator until required.

papaya salad

serves four

DRESSING

4 tbsp olive oil

1 tbsp fish sauce or light soy sauce

2 tbsp lime or lemon juice

1 tbsp dark muscovado sugar

1 tsp finely chopped fresh red or
   green chili

SALAD

1 crisp lettuce

¼ small white cabbage

2 papaya

2 tomatoes

1 oz/¼ cup roasted peanuts,
   chopped roughly

4 scallions, trimmed and sliced thinly

basil leaves, to garnish

1 To make the dressing, whisk together the oil, fish sauce or soy sauce, lime or lemon juice, sugar and chili. Set aside, stirring occasionally to dissolve the sugar.

2 Shred the lettuce and white cabbage, then toss together and arrange on a large serving plate.

3 Peel the papaya and slice them in half. Scoop out the seeds, then slice the flesh thinly. Arrange on top of the lettuce and cabbage.

4 Soak the tomatoes in a bowl of boiling water for 1 minute, then lift out and peel. Remove the seeds and chop the flesh. Arrange on the salad leaves.

5 Scatter the peanuts and scallions over the top. Whisk the dressing and pour over the salad. Garnish with basil leaves and serve at once.

citrus zing

serves four

1 pink grapefruit

1 yellow grapefruit

3 oranges

COOK'S TIP

Fruits should be heavy for their size and free from mold, mildew, bruises, cuts, or other blemishes. Some fruits are picked and shipped while still firm, so they may need additional ripening.

1 Using a sharp knife, carefully cut away all the peel and pith from the grapefruit and oranges.

2 Working over a bowl to catch the juice, carefully cut the grapefruit and orange segments between the membranes to obtain skinless segments of fruit. Discard any pips. Add the segments to the bowl and gently mix together. Cover and let chill until required or divide between 4 serving dishes and serve at once.

exotic fruit cocktail

serves four

2 oranges

2 large passion fruit

1 pineapple

1 pomegranate

1 banana

COOK'S TIP

Make sure you slice off the "eyes" when removing the skin from the pineapple.

1 Cut 1 orange in half and squeeze the juice into a bowl, discarding any pips. Using a sharp knife, cut away all the peel and pith from the second orange. Working over the bowl to catch the juice, carefully cut the orange segments between the membranes to obtain skinless segments of fruit. Discard any pips.

2 Cut the passion fruit in half, scoop the flesh into a nylon strainer and, using a spoon, push the pulp and juice into the bowl of orange segments. Discard the pips.

3 Using a sharp knife, cut away all the skin from the pineapple and cut the flesh lengthwise into quarters. Cut away the central hard core. Cut the flesh into chunks and add to the orange and passion fruit mixture. Cover and, if you are not serving at once, let the fruit chill.

4 Cut the pomegranate into quarters and, using your fingers or a teaspoon, remove the red seeds from the membrane. Cover and let chill until ready to serve—do not add too early to the fruit cocktail because the seeds discolor the other fruit.

5 Just before serving, peel and slice the banana, add to the fruit cocktail with the pomegranate seeds, and mix thoroughly. Serve at once.

pear & roquefort salad

serves four

2 oz/55 g Roquefort cheese

⅔ cup lowfat plain yogurt

2 tbsp chopped fresh chives

few leaves of lollo rosso

few leaves of radicchio

few leaves of mâche

2 ripe pears

pepper

whole fresh chives, to garnish

COOK'S TIP

Look out for bags of mixed salad greens, as these are generally more economical than buying lots of different greens separately.

1 Place the cheese in a bowl and mash with a fork. Gradually blend the yogurt into the cheese to make a smooth dressing. Add the chives and season with pepper to taste.

2 Tear the lollo rosso, radicchio, and mâche leaves into manageable pieces. Arrange the salad greens on a large serving platter or divide them between individual serving plates.

3 Cut the pears into quarters and remove the cores. Cut the quarters into slices. Arrange the pear slices over the salad leaves.

4 Drizzle the Roquefort dressing over the pears and garnish with a few whole chives.

melon & strawberry salad

½ iceberg lettuce, shredded

1 small honeydew melon

2 cups strawberries, sliced

2 inch/5 cm piece of cucumber,
    thinly sliced

fresh mint sprigs to garnish

DRESSING

scant 1 cup plain yogurt

2 inch/5 cm piece of cucumber,
    peeled

a few fresh mint leaves

½ tsp finely grated lime or lemon rind

pinch of superfine sugar

3–4 ice cubes

1 Arrange the shredded lettuce on 4 serving plates.

2 Cut the melon lengthwise into quarters. Scoop out the seeds and cut through the flesh down to the skin at 1 inch/2.5 cm intervals. Cut the melon close to the skin and detach the flesh.

3 Place the chunks of melon on the beds of lettuce with the strawberries and cucumber slices.

4 To make the dressing, put the yogurt, cucumber, mint leaves, lime or lemon rind, superfine sugar, and ice cubes into a blender or food processor. Blend together for about

15 seconds until smooth. Alternatively, chop the cucumber and mint finely, crush the ice cubes, and combine with the other ingredients.

5 Serve the salad with a little dressing poured over it. Garnish with sprigs of fresh mint.

VARIATION

Omit the ice cubes from the dressing if you prefer, but make sure that the ingredients are well-chilled. This will ensure that the finished dressing is really cool.

mango salad

serves four

1 large unripe mango, peeled and
    cut into long thin shreds

1 small fresh red chili, deseeded
    and finely chopped

2 shallots, finely chopped

2 tbsp lemon juice

1 tbsp light soy sauce

6 roasted canned chestnuts,
    quartered

1 watermelon, to serve

1 lollo biondo lettuce, or any
    crunchy lettuce

½ cup cilantro leaves

1 Soak the mango briefly in cold water, in order to remove any syrup. Meanwhile, combine the chili, shallots, lemon juice, and soy sauce. Drain the mango and combine with the chestnuts.

2 To make the melon basket, stand the watermelon on one end on a level surface. Holding a knife level and in one place, turn the watermelon on its axis so that the knife marks an even line all around the middle. Mark a 1 inch/ 2.5 cm wide handle across the top and through the center stem, joining the middle line at either end. (If you prefer a zigzag finish, mark the shape to be cut at this point before any cuts are made, to ensure an even zigzag line.)

3 Take a sharp knife and, following the marks made for the handle, make the first vertical cut. Then cut down the other side of the handle. Now follow the middle line and make your straight or zigzag cut, taking care that the knife is always pointing towards the center of the watermelon and is level with the counter, as this ensures that when you reach the handle cuts, the cut out piece of melon will pull away cleanly.

4 Hollow out the flesh with a spoon, leaving a clean edge. Line the melon basket with the lettuce and cilantro. Fill with the salad, pour over the dressing, and serve immediately.

grapefruit & coconut salad

serves four

4½ oz/1 cup grated coconut

2 tsp light soy sauce

2 tbsp lime juice

2 tbsp water

2 tsp sunflower oil

1 garlic clove, halved

1 onion, finely chopped

2 large ruby grapefruits, peeled
   and segmented

3 oz/1½ cups alfalfa sprouts

1 Toast the coconut in a dry frying skillet over a low heat, stirring constantly, for about 3 minutes, or until golden brown. Transfer the toasted coconut to a bowl.

2 Add the light soy sauce, lime juice and water to the toasted coconut and mix together well.

3 Heat the oil in a saucepan and fry the garlic and onion until soft. Stir the onion into the coconut mixture. Remove and discard the garlic.

4 Divide the grapefruit segments between 4 plates. Sprinkle each with a quarter of the alfalfa sprouts and spoon over a quarter of the coconut mixture.

COOK'S TIP
Alfalfa sprouts can be bought
in trays or packets from most
supermarkets, but you can
easily grow your own.

fresh fruit compôte

serves four

1 lemon

2 oz/¼ cup superfine sugar

4 tbsp elderflower cordial

½ pint/1¼ cups water

4 eating apples

8 oz/1 cup blackberries

2 fresh figs

TOPPING

5½ oz/⅔ cup thick unsweetened yogurt

2 tbsp clear honey

1 Thinly pare the rind from the lemon using a swivel vegetable peeler. Squeeze the juice. Put the lemon rind and juice into a saucepan, together with the sugar, elderflower cordial and water. Set over a low heat and simmer, uncovered, for 10 minutes.

2 Peel, core and slice the apples. Add the apples to the saucepan. Simmer gently for about 4–5 minutes, until just tender. Remove the pan from the heat and set aside to cool.

3 When cold, transfer the apples and syrup to a serving bowl and add the blackberries. Slice and add the figs. Stir gently to mix. Cover and chill in the refrigerator until ready to serve.

4 Spoon the yogurt into a small serving bowl and drizzle the honey over the top. Cover and chill before serving.

orchard fruits bristol

serves four

4 oranges

generous ¾ cup granulated sugar

4 tbsp water

⅔ cup white wine

4 firm pears

4 dessert apples

1 cup strawberries

1 Pare the rind thinly from 1 orange and cut into narrow strips. Cook in the minimum of boiling water for 3-4 minutes until tender. Drain and reserve the cooking liquid. Squeeze the juice from this and 1 other orange.

2 Lay a sheet of nonstick baking parchment on a cookie sheet or board.

3 Heat the sugar gently in a pan until it melts, then continue without stirring until it turns a pale golden brown. Pour half the caramel quickly onto the parchment and set aside to set.

4 Add the water and squeezed orange juice immediately to the caramel left in the pan with ⅔ cup of the reserved cooking liquid. Heat until it melts, then add the wine, and remove the pan from the heat.

5 Peel, core, and slice the pears and apples thickly (you can leave the apple skins on, if you prefer) and add to the caramel syrup. Bring gently to a boil and simmer for 3-4 minutes until just beginning to soften, they should still be firm in the center. Transfer the pears and apples to a bowl.

COOK'S TIP
The caramel will begin to melt when added to the fruit, so do this as near to serving as possible.

6 Cut away the peel and pith from the remaining oranges and either ease out the segments or cut into slices, discarding any pits. Add to the other fruits. Hull the strawberries and halve, quarter, or slice thickly, depending on the size, and add to the other fruits.

7 Add the orange strands to the syrup and bring back to a boil for 1 minute, then pour over the fruits. Set aside until cold, then break up the caramel and sprinkle it over the fruit. Cover and chill until ready to serve.

green fruit salad

serves four

1 small Charentais or Honeydew melon

2 green apples

2 kiwi fruit

4 oz/115 g seedless white grapes

fresh mint sprigs, to decorate

SYRUP

1 orange

⅔ cup white wine

⅔ cup water

4 tbsp honey

fresh mint sprigs

1 To make the syrup, pare the rind from the orange using a potato peeler.

2 Put the orange rind in a pan with the white wine, water, and honey. Bring to a boil, then simmer gently for 10 minutes.

3 Remove the syrup from the heat. Add the mint sprigs and set aside to cool.

4 To prepare the fruit, first slice the melon in half and scoop out the seeds. Use a melon baller or a teaspoon to make melon balls.

5 Core and chop the apples. Peel and slice the kiwi fruit.

6 Strain the cooled syrup into a serving bowl, removing and reserving the orange rind, and discarding the mint sprigs.

7 Add the apple, grapes, kiwi fruit, and melon to the serving bowl. Stir through gently to mix.

8 Serve the fruit salad, decorated with sprigs of fresh mint and some of the reserved orange rind.

COOK'S TIP

Single-flower honey has a better, more individual flavor than blended honey. Acacia honey is typically Chinese, but you could also try clove, lemon blossom, lime flower, or orange blossom.

peaches in white wine

serves four

4 large ripe peaches

2 tbsp confectioners' sugar, sifted

pared peel and juice of 1 orange

¾ cup medium or sweet white
  wine, chilled

1 Using a sharp knife, halve the peaches, then remove the pits and discard them. Peel the peaches, if you prefer. Slice the peaches into thin wedges.

2 Place the peach wedges in a glass serving bowl and sprinkle over the sugar.

3 Using a sharp knife, pare the peel from the orange. Cut the orange peel into short, thin sticks, then place them in a bowl of cold water and set aside.

4 Squeeze the juice from the orange and pour over the peaches together with the wine.

5 Let the peaches marinate and chill in the refrigerator for at least 1 hour.

6 Remove the orange peel from the cold water and pat dry with paper towels.

7 Garnish the peaches with the strips of orange peel and serve at once.

COOK'S TIP

The best way to pare the peel thinly from citrus fruits is to use a potato peeler.

fruit salad with ginger syrup

serves four

1 inch/2.5 cm gingerroot, peeled
   and chopped

2 oz/¼ cup caster sugar

¼ pint/⅔ cup water

grated rind and juice of 1 lime

⅓ cup/4 tbsp ginger wine

1 fresh pineapple, peeled, cored
   and cut into bite-sized pieces

2 ripe mangoes, peeled,
   stoned and diced

4 kiwi fruit, peeled and sliced

1 papaya, peeled, seeded and diced

2 passion-fruit, halved and flesh
   removed

12 oz lychees, peeled and stoned

¼ fresh coconut, grated

2 oz Cape gooseberries, to decorate
   (optional)

coconut ice-cream, to serve (optional)

1 Place the ginger, sugar, water and lime juice in a pan and bring slowly to the boil. Simmer for 1 minute, remove from the heat and allow to cool slightly.

2 Strain the syrup, add the ginger wine and mix well. Cool completely.

3 Place the prepared fruit in a serving bowl. Add the cold syrup and mix well. Cover and chill in the refrigerator for 2-4 hours.

4 Just before serving, add half of the grated coconut to the salad and mix well. Sprinkle the remainder on top.

5 If using Cape gooseberries to decorate the salad, peel back each calyx to form a flower. Wipe the berries clean, then arrange them around the side of the fruit salad before serving.

COOK'S TIP
Despite their name, Cape gooseberries are golden in colour and more similar in appearance to ground cherries. They make a delightful decoration to many fruit-based desserts.

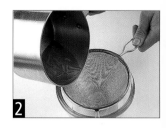

chinese fruit salad

serves four

3 fl oz/75 ml Chinese rice wine or
dry sherry

rind and juice of 1 lemon

1½ pints/850 ml water

8 oz/225 g superfine sugar

2 cloves

1-inch/2.5-cm piece cinnamon stick,
bruised

1 vanilla bean

pinch of apple pie spice

1 star anise pod

1-inch/2.5-cm piece fresh ginger
root, sliced

1¾ oz/50 g unsalted cashew nuts

2 kiwifruit

1 star fruit

4 oz/115 g strawberries

14 oz/400 g can lychees in syrup,
drained

1 piece preserved ginger, drained
and sliced

chopped mint, to decorate

COOK'S TIP

If you do need a substitute for
Chinese rice wine, pale dry sherry is
preferable to either sake (the
Japanese rice wine) or any other
cooking wines.

1 Put the Chinese rice wine or sherry, lemon rind and juice and water in a saucepan.

2 Add the superfine sugar, cloves, cinnamon stick, vanilla bean, apple pie spice, star anise and fresh gingerroot to the saucepan.

3 Heat the mixture in the pan gently, stirring constantly, until the sugar has dissolved and then bring to the boil. Reduce the heat and simmer for 5 minutes. Set aside to cool completely.

4 Strain the syrup, discarding the flavourings. Stir in the cashew nuts, cover with plastic wrap and chill in the refrigerator.

5 Meanwhile, prepare the fruits: halve and slice the kiwifruit, slice the star fruit, and hull and slice the strawberries.

6 Spoon the prepared fruit into a dish with the lychees and ginger. Stir through gently to mix.

7 Pour the syrup over the fruit, decorate with chopped mint and serve.

raspberry fusilli

serves four

6 oz/175 g fusilli pasta

4 cups raspberries

2 tbsp superfine sugar

1 tbsp lemon juice

4 tbsp slivered almonds

3 tbsp raspberry liqueur

COOK'S TIP

The raspberry liqueur provides a subtle edge to this dish. You can use any leftover liqueur in a variety of cocktails.

1 Bring a large pan of lightly salted water to a boil. Add the fusilli and cook until tender but still firm to the bite. Drain the fusilli thoroughly, return to the pan and set aside to cool.

2 Using a spoon, firmly press 1⅓ cups of the raspberries through a strainer set over a large mixing bowl to form a smooth purée.

3 Put the raspberry purée and sugar in a small pan and simmer over a low heat, stirring occasionally, for 5 minutes. Stir in the lemon juice and set the sauce aside until required.

4 Add the remaining raspberries to the fusilli in the pan and mix well. Transfer the raspberry and fusilli mixture to a serving dish.

5 Spread the almonds out on a cookie sheet and toast under the broiler until golden brown. Remove and set aside to cool slightly.

6 Stir the raspberry liqueur into the reserved raspberry sauce and mix together well until very smooth. Pour the raspberry sauce over the fusilli, then generously sprinkle over the toasted almonds and serve.

tropical fruit rice mold

serves eight

8 oz/1 cup + 2 tbsp short-grain or
   pudding rice, rinsed

1½ pints/3¾ cups skimmed milk

1 tbsp superfine sugar

4 tbsp white rum with coconut or
   unsweetened pineapple juice

6 fl oz/¾ cup lowfat natural yogurt

14 oz can pineapple pieces in natural
   juice, drained and chopped

1 tsp grated lime rind

1 tbsp lime juice

1 envelope/1 sachet powdered
   gelatine dissolved in 3 tbsp
   boiling water

lime wedges, to decorate

mixed tropical fruits such as passion-
   fruit, baby pineapple, papaya,
   mango, star fruit, to serve

1 Place the rice and milk in a
saucepan. Bring to the boil,
then simmer gently, uncovered, for
20 minutes until the rice is soft and
the milk is absorbed.

2 Stir the mixture occasionally and
keep the heat low to prevent
sticking. Transfer to a mixing bowl
and leave to cool.

3 Stir the sugar, white rum with
coconut or pineapple juice, yogurt,
pineapple pieces, lime rind and juice into
the rice. Fold into the gelatine mixture.

4 Rinse a 1.5 litre/2½ pint/1½ quart
non-stick ring mold or ring cake
pan with water and spoon in the rice
mixture. Press down well and chill for
2 hours until firm.

5 To serve, loosen the rice from the
mold with a small spatula and
invert onto a serving plate.

6 Decorate with lime wedges and
fill the center with assorted
tropical fruits.

aromatic fruit salad

serves six

1½ oz/3 tbsp granulated sugar

¼ pint/⅔ cup water

1 cinnamon stick or large piece of
cassia bark

4 cardamom pods, crushed

1 clove

juice of 1 orange

juice of 1 lime

½ Honeydew melon

a good-sized wedge of watermelon

2 ripe guavas

3 ripe nectarines

about 18 strawberries

a little toasted, shredded coconut,
for sprinkling

sprigs of mint or rose petals,
to decorate

strained unsweetened yogurt,
for serving

COOK'S TIP

Stored in a glass jar, cardamom
pods will stay fresh indefinitely.

1 First prepare the syrup. Put the sugar, water, cinnamon, cardamom pods and cloves into a pan and bring to the boil, stirring to dissolve the sugar. Simmer for 2 minutes, then remove from heat.

2 Add the orange and lime juices to the syrup and leave to cool and infuse while preparing the fruits.

3 Peel and remove the seeds from the melons and cut the flesh into neat slices.

4 Cut the guavas in half, scoop out the seeds, then peel and slice the flesh neatly.

5 Cut the nectarines into slices and hull and slice the strawberries.

6 Arrange the slices of fruit attractively on 6 serving plates.

7 Strain the prepared cooled syrup and spoon over the sliced fruits.

8 Sprinkle the fruit salad with a little toasted coconut. Decorate each serving with sprigs of mint or rose petals and serve with yogurt.

broiled fruit platter

serves ten

1 baby pineapple

1 ripe papaya

1 ripe mango

2 kiwifruit

4 finger bananas

4 tbsp dark rum

1 tsp ground allspice

2 tbsp lime juice

4 tbsp dark muscovado sugar

LIME BUTTER

2 ounces lowfat spread

½ tsp finely grated lime rind

1 tbsp confectioner's sugar

1 Quarter the pineapple, trimming away most of the leaves, and place in a shallow dish. Peel the papaya, cut it in half, and scoop out the seeds. Cut the flesh into thick wedges and place in the same dish as the pineapple.

2 Peel the mango, cut either side of the smooth, central flat pit and remove the pit. Slice the flesh into thick wedges. Peel the kiwifruit and cut in half. Peel the bananas. Add all of these fruits to the dish.

3 Sprinkle with the rum, allspice, and lime juice, cover, and leave at room temperature for 30 minutes, turning occasionally, to allow the flavors to develop.

4 Meanwhile, make the butter. Place the low-fat spread in a small bowl and beat in the lime rind and sugar until well mixed. Chill until the butter is required.

5 Preheat the broiler. Drain the fruit, reserving the juices, and arrange in the broiler pan. Sprinkle with the sugar and broil for 3-4 minutes until hot and just beginning to char.

6 Transfer the fruit to a serving plate and spoon the juices on top. Serve with the lime butter.

exotic fruit parcels

serves four

1 papaya

1 mango

1 star fruit

1 tbsp grenadine

3 tbsp orange juice

light cream or lowfat unsweetened
   yogurt, to serve

1 Cut the papaya in half, scoop out the seeds and discard them. Peel the papaya and cut the flesh into thick slices.

2 Prepare the mango by cutting it lengthwise in half either side of the central pit.

3 Score each mango half in a criss-cross pattern. Push each mango half inside out to separate the cubes and cut them away from the peel.

4 Using a sharp knife, thickly slice the star fruit.

5 Place all of the fruit in a bowl and mix them together.

6 Mix the grenadine and orange juice together and pour over the fruit. Let marinate for at least 30 minutes.

7 Divide the fruit among 4 double thickness squares of foil and gather up the edges to form a parcel that encloses the fruit.

8 Place the foil parcel on a rack set over warm coals and grill the fruit for 15-20 minutes.

9 Serve the fruit in the parcel, with the lowfat unsweetened yogurt.

rosy melon & strawberries

serves four

¼ Honeydew melon

½ Charentais or Cantaloupe melon

⅔ cup rosé wine

2–3 tsp rose water

6 oz/175 g small strawberries, washed and hulled

rose petals, to garnish

1 Scoop out the seeds from both melons with a spoon. Then carefully remove the skin, taking care not to remove too much flesh.

2 Cut the melon flesh into thin strips and place in a bowl. Pour over the wine and sufficient rose water to taste. Stir the melon and the liquid together gently to combine, cover, and let chill in the refrigerator for at least 2 hours.

3 Halve the strawberries and carefully mix them into the macerated melon. Let the melon and strawberries stand at room temperature for about 15 minutes for the flavors to develop before serving—if the melon is served too cold, there will be little flavor.

4 Arrange the melon and strawberries on individual serving plates and serve sprinkled with a few rose petals.

balsamic strawberries

1 lb/450 g fresh strawberries

2–3 tbsp balsamic vinegar

fresh mint leaves, torn, plus extra
    to decorate (optional)

½–¾ cup mascarpone cheese

pepper

COOK'S TIP

This is most enjoyable when it is
made with the best-quality
balsamic vinegar, one that
has aged slowly and has turned
thick and syrupy. Unfortunately,
the genuine mixture is always
expensive. Less expensive
versions are artificially
sweetened and colored
with caramel.

1 Wipe the strawberries with a damp cloth, rather than rinsing them, so they do not become soggy. Using a paring knife, cut off the green stalks at the top and use the tip of the knife to remove the core or hull.

2 Cut each strawberry in half lengthwise or into quarters if large. Transfer to a bowl.

3 Add the balsamic vinegar, allowing ½ tablespoon per person. Add several twists of ground black pepper, then gently stir together. Cover with plastic wrap and chill for up to 4 hours.

4 Just before serving, stir in torn mint leaves to taste. Spoon the mascarpone into bowls and spoon the berries on top. Decorate with a few mint leaves, if wished. Sprinkle with extra pepper to taste.